Grace Overcomers Addiction Ministry is more than just pages of good spiritual sense and instruction. It is the result of a man living and revealing to others the grace life…vital for raising men out of the dunghill and showing them their great value and potential in God's plan for their lives.

—Pastor David Stambovsky

Your book *Grace Overcomers Addiction Ministry* found its way all the way to our counter in Pacific Beach, Washington. It sat there for a month or so, and then my wife and I started reading it. What a book! I'm going to forward it to another relative when we are finished with it. My wife has been reading parts of it out loud to me. Thank you for sending it to me!

—Arthur Egeli, fine artist/award winning filmmaker

Through *Grace Overcomers Addictions Ministry* and Pastor Dan Lightsey, many lives will be deeply touched. The testimonies in this book show the power of God's grace to change a life. People who were once lost in "a wilderness experience" are now living in their intended position in Christ "seated above in heavenly places." My husband is such a miracle of grace. I thank God that he has used such a humble servant as Pastor Lightsey to reach out to those who are struggling with addiction in such a doctrinally sound and powerful way. It is my prayer that all who read this book will come to experience God's plan for their lives in a deeper way than they ever thought possible.

—Vera B. Brown, M.D.

GRACE
OVERCOMERS
ADDICTION MINISTRY

GRACE
OVERCOMERS
ADDICTION MINISTRY

Founded on the Finished
Work of Jesus Christ

DAN LIGHTSEY

Tate Publishing & Enterprises

Grace Overcomers Addiction Ministry
Copyright © 2010 by Dan Lightsey. All rights reserved.

No part of this publication may be reproduced, stored in a retrieval system or transmitted in any way by any means, electronic, mechanical, photocopy, recording or otherwise without the prior permission of the author except as provided by USA copyright law.

Scripture quotations are taken from the *Holy Bible, King James Version,* Cambridge, 1769. Used by permission. All rights reserved.

This is a work of nonfiction. Names, descriptions, entities, and incidents included in the story are based on the lives of real people.

This book is designed to provide accurate and authoritative information with regard to the subject matter covered. This information is given with the understanding that neither the author nor Tate Publishing, LLC is engaged in rendering legal, professional advice. Since the details of your situation are fact dependent, you should additionally seek the services of a competent professional.

The opinions expressed by the author are not necessarily those of Tate Publishing, LLC.

Published by Tate Publishing & Enterprises, LLC
127 E. Trade Center Terrace | Mustang, Oklahoma 73064 USA
1.888.361.9473 | www.tatepublishing.com

Tate Publishing is committed to excellence in the publishing industry. The company reflects the philosophy established by the founders, based on Psalm 68:11,
"The Lord gave the word and great was the company of those who published it."

Book design copyright © 2009 by Tate Publishing, LLC. All rights reserved.
Cover design by Kellie Southerland
Interior design by Jeff Fisher

Published in the United States of America

ISBN: 978-1-61663-225-0
1. Self-Help, Substance Abuse & Addictions, General
2. Religion, Christian Ministry, Counseling & Recovery
10.04.26

DEDICATION

This book is written by and for Grace Overcomers in their own words with names deleted to honor the doctrine of confidentiality.

Dedicated to our pastor, the late Dr. Carl H. Stevens Jr. Without his wise counsel and sound teaching, this book would not have been possible.

ACKNOWLEDGMENTS

Thanks to my wife, Sandra Lightsey, who has loved, helped, and encouraged me in this ministry all these many years. We also thank our pastor, Thomas Schaller, for continuing to inspire us in the furtherance of the Gospel; Bruce and Sue May of Grace Publications; and Steve Andrulonis for submitting this work to Tate. Our thanks to Tony and Ann Marie Pallotta, Fred and Leah Ellis, Tony and Vera Brown, Bob and Chris Colban, Rob Pinkava, and other team members too numerous to name. May God bless, and we thank you all.

"No Cross, No Crown"

The cross is the crux of the universe,

And the epitome of wisdom;

The fulcrum on which truth rests and turns.

While knaves twist, and fools resist its simplicity;

Philosophical isms, and jazzmen's riffs,

Religious schisms, and Kipling's ifs,

Are swallowed by its profundity.

And without the cross

There can be no crown.

TABLE OF CONTENTS

Foreword 13

Introductory Statement of Faith and Purpose 15

Sweet Supreme (A Poem) 19

1. An Honest Look at the Problem:
   The Blame Game 21

2. All are Addicted to Something 27
   The Power of Grace (Testimony) 28
   All Washed Up (Testimony) 31

3. Our Experience in Twelve-step Groups 33
   A Step of Faith (Testimony) 38
   Faithful Is He Who Called Us (Testimony) 40
   Only Christ Can Truly Satisfy (Testimony) 44

4. A Temporary Dwelling Place 47

5. Forty Years in the Wilderness (Testimony) 51
   Thank You, Jesus, for Setting Me Free (Testimony) . . . 54

6. Circumcision of the Heart 67

7. From the Gutter to Glory
   by the Grace of God (Testimony) 73

8	Positive Volition and the New Position	77
	I Don't Do That Anymore (Testimony)	79
	A New Self-Image, a New Life, and a New Purpose (Testimony)	81
9.	The Enemy is Pride	85
	Satan's Limited Authority	89
10.	Ultimately It Is God Who Changes Behavior	93
11.	The Role of the Local Church in Recovery from Addiction	97
12.	What God can Do with Damages Goods (Testimony)	103
	My Prize (A Poem)	107
13.	How God, With Our Cooperation, Works	109
	Seven Principles or Pillars of Wisdom	110
	Seven Revelatory Principles	125
	Set on Fifteen Foundational Bedrocks	125

Appendix ... 131

Seven Precepts ... 131

Addict's Prayer ... 135

Bibliography ... 137

FOREWORD

It is refreshing both to the addict and to the counselor to look at addictions head-on. Train wrecks, diseases, and addictions have to be dealt with in real terms. It would be dishonest to sidestep the need for real acknowledgment and accountability. But who will ultimately deliver and guide us?

Christ has been manifested in the world again and again as the one who is the same yesterday, today, and forever. The local church, the Word of God, and the work of the Holy Spirit are able to lead and guide him in complete and permanent deliverance. He has a new life.

Study the elements presented in this book. Testimonies of these believers smack of the genuine transformation that is available for all of us. I believe whoever is seeking the real God will find Him. He will speak to you, He will guide you, and yes, He will deliver you and give you an eternal purpose.

I particularly enjoyed the chapter on "The Role of the Local Church in the Recovery from Addiction." This teaching should never be overlooked. It is critical for our deliverance and continuance in victory. Many fall back and do not continue on because they lack the ministry of the local assembly. The assembly will teach, comfort, enlighten, encourage, and motivate us. It is the missing link in permanent recovery. It is awesomely exciting.

Pastor Dan Lightsey has the transformed life and years of experience in counseling. He is a gracious, hard-hitting, and gentle man who loves people. We all know that we have no real solution for life outside of Christ and His people. We have a real enemy, but we also have a real friend. We also have the friends of the one real and true Friend.

Read and rejoice in what God can do for your life. Attend, faithfully and consistently, the local assembly under God-given anointed preaching. It will revolutionize your life. Christ has given you a new life.

—Pastor Thomas Schaller

INTRODUCTORY STATEMENT OF FAITH AND PURPOSE

What is Grace Overcomers?

Grace Overcomers is an addiction ministry and an outreach of the local church. We are made up of men and women, who, by childlike faith in the finished work victory, given to us by our Lord Jesus Christ, have overcome. And in a growth process of His grace and knowledge, we are overcoming negative thinking and addictive behavior patterns. In times past, those patterns of enslavement brought on spiritual death. Ultimately, had they not been broken, they would have resulted in physical death (Mark 10:15; John 17:4, 19:30; 1 Corinthians 15:57; Revelation 2:7, 12:10–11; John 5:4–5; Proverbs 23:1–35, 24:9; Psalm 68:6, 107:10–13; Acts 8:23; Romans 8:6; Isaiah 10:27; 1 John 5:16).

Based on a reasonable presupposition, an exegetical search of the Scriptures, we trust in a God who cannot lie, and having been taught the truth in faith and verity, we are certain of the things wherein we have been instructed. These having proven true in our lives, we sit before you clean and sober, living epistles of that veracity and grace. Though still sinners, we are mirroring His likeness. Therefore, we do state without equivocation that the Bible is the Word of God written by the prophets of old, inspired by the Holy Spirit, not open to private interpretation, but is to be rightly divided and literally interpreted according to original language, historical setting, and dispensational truth (Isaiah 1:18–20; John 5:39; Acts 17:11; Numbers 23:19; Titus 1:1; Hebrews 6:18; 1 Timothy 2:7; Luke 1:4; 2 Corinthians 3:1–18; John 1:1; 2 Timothy 3:16; 2 Peter 1:20; 2 Timothy 2:15; 1 Corinthians 9:17; Ephesians 1:10, 3:2).

In faith obedience to the great commission and motivated by the divine commandment, which says we are to love the Lord with our heart, soul, and mind and our neighbor (the struggling addict) as ourselves, we do not then commend, nor do we live unto ourselves; but he, having made us "sober for your cause," compels us to proclaim the message of a new life, recovery, and reconciliation (Hebrews 11:8; Matthew 28:16–20; Mark 16:14–20; Luke 24:36–48; John 21:1–25; Mark 12:33; 2 Corinthians 5:12–18).

Our purpose then, in union with Him, is the bringing of many sons and daughters (the addicted) to the glory of Jesus Christ, in so doing, reminding ourselves that He perfected our salvation through His suffering.

If it be that you have a willing mind, a broken heart, and a contrite spirit, incline your ear, listen, read on, come to the waters of His Word, and your soul shall be healed (Hebrews 2:10; 2 Corinthians 8:12; Psalms 18, 52:16–17; Isaiah 55:1–3).

Why write a book?

Initially we spent five years in the writing and research for the original *Grace Overcomers* manuscript. Using a self-bound spiral binder and copy machine, we came up with 100 copies. With the expertise of Tate Publishing and their channels of distribution, we hope to reach a wider readership. Thanks to Tate for taking on the project.

Our success is reflected in the testimonies you will read in the book. These and numerous other individuals have been touched by God through Grace Overcomers ministry. Some have been ordained and are pastoring local churches. Others are, or have been, missionaries on the foreign field. While I, Pastor Dan Lightsey, am the founder of the ministry, the author of the commentary and scriptural compilations, and editor of the testimonies throughout the book—my own included, in chapter 5—I use *us* and *we* in these writings. None of it would have been possible without the prayerful unction of the Holy Spirit, and the help of the faithful team members over the years. Thank you all!

Our hope in seeking an international readership for *Grace Overcomers Addictions Ministry,* the book, is primarily to reach the lost—from convicts in prison cells to professors and students in colleges and seminaries, judges and probation officers, and distraught parents whose children are using drugs. And yes, to the homeless and heartbroken, there is hope in Jesus Christ. All scriptural references and citations are taken from the King James Version. However, we often use the Amplified Bible when teaching in our meetings. We find it is easier to understand and closer to the original language. *Grace Overcomers Addictions Ministry,* the book, is unique in that we have not found anything—either in Christian Recovery or the 12-step model circles—like it. It is set up in a simple and concise format so as to be easy to carry and understand. Using this book with its memory keys, Seven Principles and Fifteen Foundational Bedrocks, as a companion to the Scriptures, any individual is able to apply Bible doctrine to their lives, thus transforming the soul.

Whether one has an addiction problem or a sin problem, they are one in the same. May you find rest for your soul.

The Seven Precepts in the back of the book are guidelines for setting up a Grace Overcomers Ministry in the local church. We hope you will do so! See our website: www.graceovercomers.org.

SWEET SUPREME

In years past, we looked to the stars for our fortune,
Strobes and crystals, for light;
Sought direction in the spin of a wheel,
Looked to the turn of a card, for sight.
Seeking seers for wisdom
And philosophers for truth,
We had a dream at the end of the darkest night,
Of our misspent youth.
We dreamt we were in His arms,
Felt His gentle embrace;
Out of harm's way,
Looking full in His wonderful face.
Upon awakening to a new day,
Heads were clear, hearts were free,
Spirits clean.
For you see, Jesus Christ,
Had shed His light, Sweet Supreme.
We had walked in ignorance,
Chasing fiery comets.
We were so blind, living an existence.
Never cared to go to the distance;
Never thought we'd find solace in
Our Sweet Lord, our Sweet Supreme.
He lifted the weight of our earthly burdens.
He's healed our souls;
We're no longer hurting.
Oh such joy!
Nothing can destroy
Our faith in the Word of Sweet Supreme
We're so grateful for His love;
His grace makes us whole.
We've felt His gentle touch.
It's not a dream, sweet Jesus.
He's coming back soon,
Sweet Supreme.

CHAPTER 1

*An Honest Look at the Problem:
The Blame Game*

In the keeping of our purpose, we have made some observations and drawn some conclusions. In the course of our search for answers in our own lives, we found that, although each of us was a unique individual, there were certain things that we had in common.

For example: genetics. Many of our parents and some of our close relatives had addiction problems. Some of us lacked infant nurturing, due to the loss of a mother. The instability or absence of a father was often a factor. In some cases, we were victims of physical, verbal, and sexual abuse, by which we were traumatized as children. These traumatic experiences sometimes left us with unresolved guilt, and in many cases, deep anger.

Peer pressure, the extent of our education, and what neighborhood we grew up in all had an effect. They were some of the things that were instrumental in the forming of our character and the shaping of our personalities. The barrage of stories on the printed pages of newspapers and magazines that came from Madison Avenue and Main Street had an effect on our thinking.

Music, art, and the visual images projected on movie and TV screens influenced us. The stars of these, athletes in sporting events, and sometimes the slicksters on the corner became our heroes. We lived in a fantasy, emulating the celebrated and the infamous, only to discover that in many cases they were as confused and addicted as we were. Upon finding this out, we used this information to reinforce our addictive lifestyles.

The world system, or *cosmos diabolicus* that promotes peace of mind through prosperity and affluence through achievement drove us. It left us frustrated with poor self-images when we did not measure up, or briefly elated, though always needing another conquest to boost our egos when we did make the grade (1 John 5:19; James 4:4).

Our religious training, or lack of it, caused us to form concepts that were not easily broken. Most of us looked back at our circumstances. In need of a scapegoat because we found it too painful to accept responsibility for our own failures, we blamed God, the church, our parents, and authority figures for the problems that plagued us.

What Part Did the Devil Play?

Addiction is the result of idolatrous (or sinful) behavior. There is no doubt that we were influenced by evil, for wherever "the devil is given place" through idolatry, his demonic hosts play on the mind (Ephesians 4:27).

According to the Bible, "Idolatry is rebellion, and is as the sin of witchcraft" Synonymous with the word *witchcraft* are the words *sorcery* and in the *Vine's Exposi-*

tory Dictionary of New Testament Words, pharmakos. It is, and I quote, "An adjective signifying devotion to magical arts. When used as a noun it means sorcerer, especially one who uses drugs, potions, spells or enchantments" Sorcery and drunkenness are listed in the Bible as the "works of the flesh" (1 Samuel 15:23; Revelation 21:8, 22:15; Galatians 5:20–21).

The word *pharmakia,* from which the English word *pharmacy* is derived, primarily signifies the use of medicine, drugs, spells, and poisonings. Hence, one will see a skull and crossbones on the bottles from which the modern-day druggist dispenses opiates and cocaine. In ancient times, and even today, in some third world countries, certain psychedelic potions and hypnotic practices have been touted as being a protection to ward off evil spirits. In modern times, the purveyor of drugs promises to cure whatever ails us, from boredom and loneliness to fatigue and depression, while he tempts us to try his wares. The ads of brewers, distillers, and tobacco companies equate beauty, sophistication, and sexual potency with the use of their products. They imply that we will be successful in our romantic conquests if we use whatever it is they are selling.

Vine's Dictionary further cites Isaiah 47:9–15 and Revelation 9:21 and 18:23 to point out the wholesale deception and the end result of individuals and nations who continue these practices by using ancient and modern-day Babylon as examples. We would only have to read recent history regarding China, where opiate addiction was rampant, or visit Haiti, where witchcraft is prevalent, to see that this is true. The rise in addiction over the past thirty years in the United States has corrupted our nation to the core. This diabolic trend coincides with the legalization of abortion and the removal of prayer from public schools.

We are all influenced by some or all the aforementioned factors and are well able to rationalize the circumstances that caused us to make the choices that led to addiction. Still, it was our choice to be a liar, a thief, a drug addict, or to a greater or lesser degree, whatever we had become. In order to flourish, our addiction was dependent on our living in deception, willfulness, and shades of unbelief. It could not have continued to exist without our full cooperation. While we may have entered into it thinking that it would provide something good, we soon found ourselves in bondage to people, behavior, and substances.

According to the late Dr. Lewis Sperry Chafer, in volume seven of his work *Systematic Theology:* "The will is subject to various influences and is either under the sovereign control of God, if saved and if not, under the control of Satan" (Philippians 2:13; Ephesians 2:2). If we, though saved because of grace and our profession of faith are not walking by faith in the filling of the Holy Spirit purposing in our hearts to "live by every Word of God" on a daily basis and confessing sin to the Father when we fail, we are subject to demonic influence (2 Corinthians 5:7; Ephesians 5:18; Matthew 4:4; 1 John 1:9). That is why some Christians continue in addiction for years after they are saved. They are afraid to trust God for their deliverance, which was accomplished on their behalf at the cross.

Negative Volition and the Fallen Condition

In simple terms, the problem we had as addicts, (were we chemical abusers, pornography viewers, overt sexual deviants, compulsive gamblers, overeaters, workaholics, or those who sought power through the control and manipulation of people), was sin. Having inherited an 'old sin nature," our predisposition was to go astray (Psalm 51:5; Isaiah 53:5–6). We sought to fulfill our desires at any cost. Rather than going to God, we entered into behavior patterns and the partaking of substances that either heightened or dulled our senses. We sought fulfillment through the lust of the eyes (we saw it, and it looked good) the lust of the flesh (physically we craved it, thought we had to have it, and thus, after we had partaken of it, we were corrupted by it), and the pride of life (either directly or indirectly we thought it would improve our circumstances) (Genesis 3:6; Galatians 6:8; Proverbs 16:18; Jeremiah 49:16). We labored under the illusion that we would be satisfied with the right combination of the addictive substance or just a little more. Needless to say, satisfaction never came (Proverbs 27:20, 30:5; Ecclesiastes 5:10). The substance we abused and the behaviors we entered into were created and instituted by God for good in their own time and in His purpose (Genesis 1:31; Ecclesiastes 3:1).

Drugs have medical purposes. Food is for nourishment. Sex in marriage brings pleasure and procreation. But we found that outside of his order, these things could, and often did, devastate us. Yet, because of ignorance, fear, insecurity, and selfishness, we rebelled against God and passionately pursued these things. They seemed to give us pleasure, calming our nerves, relieving stress, and temporarily easing our pain (Hebrews 11:25).

In the process of seeking relief, we became enslaved by the things we thought would free us. When we had really gotten honest, we found that they were not all that they had been "cracked up" to be. (Pun intended!) Ultimately, we were the product of a series of negative volitional choices, at the root of which was a fallen condition, common to all in the human race (Genesis 3:6; Isaiah 1:5, 64:6; Jeremiah 17:9; Romans 3:10, 3:23).

CHAPTER 2

All Are Addicted to Something

Or Is it, "All Have Sinned and Come Short of God's Glory"?

In his book entitled *Addiction and Grace,* psychiatrist Gerald G. May defines *addiction* as being "the attachment coming from the old French word *attaché,* which when translated, means nailing of desire." He writes, "While repression stifles desire, addiction nails, bonds, and enslaves the energy of desire to certain specific behavior, things, or people."

According to Dr. May, "traditional psychotherapy, which is based on the release of repression, has proven ineffective in the treatment of the addict. Addiction is the most powerful psychic enemy of humanity's desire for God."

He states, "There are three very real components present in the mind of the addict: self-deception, denial, and rationalization. These result in the setting up of defense mechanisms to hide and avoid dealing with the problem."

He likens the addiction process unto "the old testament journey of the Israelites through the wilderness of idolatry, where temptations, trials, and deprivation abounds, but where the grace of God is always available to guide, protect, empower, and transform the addicted person."

He bases these findings on years of research while working with the chemically dependent. In the course of his work, he found that he too was addicted to a variety of substances and behaviors. While they were far less harmful than those of the heroin addict or alcoholic, they were nevertheless a hindrance in his life, and, in the case of tobacco, could cause cancer and even be fatal. Essentially, his unfulfilled desires left him spiritually bankrupt, causing him to pray in childlike faith, "Dear Jesus, help me."

He concludes by saying, "the human race is driven by obsessive thinking and compulsive behavior, and all are addicted to something, but by grace, faith, and the exercise of free will, addiction can be overcome."

What follows are testimonies that lend credence to what has been said thus far, along with commentary drawn from the well of our experiences.

The Power of Grace (Testimony)

This testimony is truly one of God's grace and particularly of His power. If it were not for this grace, I probably wouldn't be alive today! My life was marked by the desire to achieve; however, always present was a weakness in accomplishment.

As I grew up in the social unrest of the 1960s and '70s, I was confused by the apparent injustice in our world. Seeking to establish an identity, which is a process all adolescents go through, I began to succumb to peer pressure and rebel against the authority of my parents. Substance abuse began in my life at the age of fourteen, when I started drinking vodka on weekends. At the time of my father's death several years later, I began using drugs. Somehow I resented my father for having died. Pot, hash, speed, and whatever was available, I tried. My life was on the road of destruction without much hope of change. Eventually, I tried heroin, and it immediately became my drug of choice. It seemed to comfort my soul, bringing a false sense of peace to my mind and a rest to my body. As with all of Satan's deceptions, this high came at a great price, causing pain to my family, loss of true friends, and anguish to me.

As tolerance for the drug grew, my habit became more difficult to support. Before long, I began dealing drugs. After two felony arrests, I decided it was time to seek professional help. Methadone programs were becoming popular in the early '70s, so I got involved in one of those. Methadone seemed to control my addiction for a while, but when the initial effect wore off, I was left unsatisfied. As a result, I found myself using a higher dose of heroin, along with other drugs, in an attempt to get relief. My next step was to go inpatient at the Veteran's Hospital in Boston. I was able to stay there for four months, drug free. Outwardly I was cured, but inwardly, I was still an addict. Upon leaving the hospital, my sobriety lasted all of one day. My inability to overcome the addiction to drugs was becoming more apparent. These events brought me to the power of God's grace.

One day, an old friend of mine came by the house to talk to me. He had recently accepted Christ. He told me, "What you need is to get to know Jesus as your personal Savior. He will give you the power to overcome your addiction." My response was, "Yeah, sure, so what kind of high are you into now?"

As time went on, he kept coming by and continued to share the gospel with me. One day, while he was reading a passage from the Bible aloud, the Holy Spirit spoke to my heart. I knew at that moment that I had been changed forever!

The week following this event, I went to the methadone clinic and told my counselor to put me on a quick detox schedule. He looked at me in disbelief, for he was very familiar with my history of past failures.

He said, "You were just in here last week asking for an increase in your dose of methadone." To which I responded, "Yes, that is true, but I am no longer that man. I now have Jesus Christ in my life, and He has made me a brand-new person." He very reluctantly put me on a two-week detox regimen. This was, by standard program practices, a ridiculously short amount of time for someone who had been addicted for a number of years.

Two weeks later, much to the surprise of my doctor, my counselor, my family, and perhaps even myself, I was clean and sober for the first time in many years. I am writing this testimony to the power of God's grace with the hope and expectation that the same truth that set me free will be received and experienced by others who are struggling with addiction. My involvement with Grace Overcomers has helped me to know God in many new areas of my life. It has also given me the opportunity to share the provision of His grace with others. It has now been more than fifteen years since this took place. I am married with three children, and I am still trusting in the words of our Lord Jesus Christ when He said, "My grace is sufficient for thee: for my strength is made perfect in weakness" (2 Corinthians 12:9). This is the power of grace!

All Washed Up (Testimony)

As a little boy growing up, I will never forget my grandmother reading the Scriptures to me. "Come unto me, all ye that labor and are heavy laden, and I will give you rest." And she continued, "Take my yoke upon you, and learn of me; for I am meek and lowly in heart: and ye shall find rest unto your souls" (Matthew 11:28–29).

It seemed to me she had the entire Bible committed to memory. "What is a yoke, Grandma?" I would ask her.

"A yoke is a collar, son," she would patiently state, "that is put on a beast of burden to make 'em behave. It is either a well-oiled, wooden yoke put on by a gentle taskmaster or a yoke of iron used by the slave masters. Jesus is a gentle taskmaster, little son," she would say sweetly.

Oh, how it grieved my grandmother, the look on her face, when she caught me smoking a cigarette out behind the house. I was seventeen at the time and well beyond the first experience phase of the deadly nicotine habit. So the journey began, smoking, drinking, and doing drugs. Finally, I was introduced to crack cocaine.

Early on, I was able to hold a job and function in some semblance of normalcy. Within a matter of months, though, I had become a lying, stealing, conniving fool. What my brokenhearted grandmother had seen in me years before had become a reality. Homeless and in bondage, my yoke of iron was crack cocaine, and the devil was my taskmaster. My life was out of control, and I was in a state of denial for a very long time.

My most memorable encounter with the Lord was in a public restroom connected to a deserted laundromat at 3:00 a.m. I sought refuge there to partake of my last rock of crack. What I encountered when I turned on the light was an indescribable filth and a stench that filled my nostrils. It was as though a person had blown up in there and their innards had been splattered upon the walls. However, my craving for cocaine took precedence over the repulsion that I experienced. At that moment, I had a revelation of my heart as "deceitful and desperately wicked" (Jeremiah 17:9). I did not know myself. Like the prodigal son, I came to myself, knowing that the life I had been living was not what God had intended for me. He met me in that horrible restroom and ironically began cleaning me up in the laundromat.

Since that time, I have graduated from Bible college, gotten married to a beautiful woman, and am the father of two sweet children. My heart's desire in writing this testimony is to remind myself, like the prodigal son and so many others, that we can find our way home. Like the Apostle Paul said, "While we were yet sinners, Christ died for us" (Romans 5:8). His name is Jesus, and He is "the way, the truth, and the life" (John 14:6).

CHAPTER 3

Our Experience in Twelve-step Groups

Many of us have spent countless hours in Alcoholics and Narcotics Anonymous. Some of us began our sobriety there and do still attend meetings. While we do not depend upon those meetings for our ongoing sobriety, our dependence is upon Jesus Christ. We attend so that we may reach out to those who do not know Him.

When we go, we are there as His ambassadors (2 Corinthians 5:20). Before we proceed, we would like to acknowledge and thank those who were there in the rooms for us, in some instances, when everyone else had given up hope—the Andys, Johnnies, Richards, Toms, Teds, Phyllises, Alices, and Janes, along with those too numerous to name, who drove the extra miles and carried the hot cups of coffee. It is because of people such as these that many drunks and drug addicts no longer get behind the wheel of a car while under the influence and no longer beat their wives or abuse and neglect their children. Their lives, jobs, and the tax dollars that have been saved through their acts of kindness are many and have been profitable to society. The benefits of these programs, in that sense, cannot be measured.

Unfortunately, getting dried out and becoming responsible does not save one's soul. For the Bible says, "For what is a man profited, if he shall gain the whole world, and lose his own soul? Or what shall a man give in exchange for his soul?" (Matthew 16:26). Thank God for the Lamars, the late Harold Hill, and the other twelve-steppers who do lead people to a saving knowledge of Jesus Christ in the car or over coffee after a meeting. The Pastor Bills, who as one of our stories will tell, rebuked our rebelliousness and challenged us to get right and go on with God. Where would we be today if not for their being in the rooms of A.A. and N.A. meetings?

In order to honestly assess the overall effectiveness of the twelve-step movement, we must go back to its origin. It started as a splinter of the Oxford Group, which was a Christian ministry to alcoholics in the mid-1930s. After much debate and conjecture, and in preparation for the publication of the first A.A. book, which ironically was published by Works Publishing Company, it was decided that any reference to Jesus Christ in the text of the twelve-steps would be deleted. This was done by coming up with the expression, "God as we understood him," so as to make the message more palatable to the atheist, the agnostic, and those of other non-Christian persuasions. This was done to not be offensive. It was thought that, being offended, those needing help would leave the meeting and thus die as hopeless drunks (see *A.A Comes of Age,* an A.A World Services Publication).

As sincere as these folks may have been in their effort, were they right or sincerely wrong?

It was also felt by the shapers and formers of the twelve-steps that a purely biblical formula with a Christ-centered message was too authoritarian and too religious in content. Departing from the sincere milk of God's Word, their intent was to spoonfeed those in early recovery with a generic form of spiritual pablum that would be acceptable to all(1 Peter 2:2). The question becomes, from what spirit is it derived? It was thought that alcoholics, who had been victimized by authority figures, were turned off by preachers with messages of condemnation, or found church services boring because of ritual, and had rebelled for reasons either real or imaginary, would eventually come around.

Since the founders were not evangelical and were able to eventually get the endorsements of a Catholic priest and a protestant minister, along with medical doctors, this makes sense. In some cases, especially early on in A.A., this formula had the effect of getting people dried out, and many recognized the higher power as the God of their childhood and were converted, returning either to the denomination they were familiar with or a comparable church of their choosing. Some of us were in that category. However, more times than not, people in the rooms of A.A., and especially N.A, have made the group their church or lodge. Working the twelve-steps in a systematic religious manner, along with the twelve traditions, they have made these writings their commandments and the big book their Bible. The higher power or god of the understanding is either a group conscience or, since there are never any absolutes taught, it is left open to private interpretation (see 2 Peter 1:20).

Because natural or unregenerate persons, with their understanding being darkened by the fall "cannot receive the things of God" the god of their understanding is subject to their own whims, or whatever doctrine that happens to be blowing in the wind (Ephesians 4:14, 4:18; Genesis 3:6; 1 Corinthians 2:14). Contrary to what popular culture says, the answer is not "blowing in the wind."

In this instance, because they may no longer be drinking or doing drugs and even generating good works, there is a form a godliness but a denial of the source of real power (2 Timothy 3:5). The same denial mechanism that was at work in addiction causes spiritual deception in this instance. Because "the heart is deceitful and desperately wicked," we cannot know ourselves (Jeremiah 17:9). Left to one's own vain imaginations, the perception of God becomes distorted (2 Corinthians 10:5). The French philosopher, Voltaire, once said, "God created man in his own image, and man has been attempting to recreate God in his own image ever since."

When motives are subject to a selfish agenda, the tendency is to live in the comfort of error. Those people who do not want to face the cross of Christ tend to embrace new age doctrines—doctrines which are not new at all, but are age old "doctrines of devils" or doctrines of men (1 Timothy 4:1; Colossians 2:22). Outside of objective biblical truth and the regeneration of the heart and mind, which can only come through the "new birth", the higher power can become an angel of (spiritual enlightenment) light and the god of our understanding carries the danger of becoming pantheistic (John 3:3; 2 Corinthians 11:14).

For example, in the course of a group discussion, people will identify their higher power as being a tree or some other inanimate object, anything to avoid accountability to a personal God. The problem people have with the God of the Bible is that He is too specific. The natural or unregenerate person, as well as the carnal Christian, is at enmity, or opposition, with God and hates to deal with Him in specifics. He or she would rather keep God locked up in a conceptual box, making Him, a being of abstract ideation, anything but who He really is: the God of love, grace, and mercy, who died for the sins of all.

In the book of Exodus (chapter 20, verses 25–26), God instructs the people how to make an altar. He says, "It is not to be of hewn stone; for if thou lift up a tool upon it, thou hast polluted it, neither shalt thou go up by steps to thine altar." The New Testament correlations to this truth are: "Works do not save us, nor do they justify us" and it is "not by works of righteousness which we have done, but according to his mercy, by the washing of the regeneration, and renewing through the Holy Spirit" that we are saved (Ephesians 2:9; Galatians 2:16; Titus 3:5). Jesus Christ, who "is God" "made himself of no reputation, and took upon him the form of a servant, and was made in the likeness of men: and being found in fashion as a man, he humbled himself, and became obedient unto death, even the death of the cross" (John 1:1; Philippians 2:7–8). Coming down to our level "He glorified the Father by finishing the work" in behalf of the entire human race(Matthew 11:29; John 17:4). The only prerequisite for a spiritual awakening is that we believe his words and accept Him (John 17:8). God's is a one-step program: simply believe.

Here is what happened to a nurse when she did just that. Believed!

A Step of Faith (Testimony)

Taking a step of faith, I accepted Jesus Christ as my personal Savior in January of 1987. Around that time, my husband and I had started going to a Bible study in Stoneham, Massachusetts. Recognizing our addiction problem, we had been attending A.A. meetings regularly. God used people in the meeting as examples of sober living, but all the slogans left us questioning who this higher power really was.

I spent much of my life looking for someone to love me, yet I was never satisfied with the love I received from my parents, friends, or the men in my life. I married early, thinking that my husband would fulfill me, but something was always missing.

Along with attending nursing school, I tried some self-achievement programs. Upon graduation, I was licensed and got a job at the local hospital. Still, I was left feeling empty. I had been introduced to alcohol, pot, and pills earlier in my teenage years and found myself becoming more and more dependent on these chemicals as time went on. I would lie to my family, friends, and supervisors at work in an attempt to cover my drug use. Promiscuous sexual relationships left me empty and plagued with guilt.

Finally, I was introduced to cocaine, and it became my best friend. In the end, it left me lonely, sick, tired, and hopelessly depressed.

Getting on my knees one day, I asked God for help. Things quickly became unbearable. Cocaine was making me physically and emotionally sick. Each time I got high, instead of feeling better, I felt worse. It got so bad that I could no longer work. People were avoiding me, and I was hurting terribly.

Then one day, my mom and dad showed up and took me home with them. My prayer was being answered. At their coaxing, I signed myself into the hospital detox unit. That's where I began a new life with God in control. I didn't get it all right away, but little by little the Holy Spirit started a work in me. All I had to offer was a little willingness.

Since that time, God has healed me to the point that I no longer even recall some of the things that I used to do. He has "restored to me the years the locust has eaten" (Joel 2:25). I now have the life that I had been looking for all along. I don't have a perfect life, but the life that I live is perfect because of He who lives it in me. The man I married was searching for love also, and we have found it together. It is the right kind of love, that which never fails. Between us is the love of Jesus Christ; and because He is in control of our lives, we can be kind, giving grace to one another for the situations He orders for us daily.

As we experience our new life in Christ, the incredible emptiness which haunted us in the past is now gone. The void has been filled. We have a loving family that includes a son who is growing into a young man that loves God, along with a three-year-old boy, whom I can be there for because I am alert and responsible today.

My husband, who was also an addict, is now sober and hard working. He ministers the Word of God in our home and heads up a weekly Grace Overcomers meeting. Through receiving biblical teaching from our pastor and fellowship in the body of Christ (local church), we now live in the eternal is of His presence, instead of the fears and anxiety of our past. We know to be happy and fulfilled is to live according to His Word. Today we depend on God, not drugs. Our faith in Jesus Christ is causing us to grow in His grace and knowledge. In the process, we experience His love and mercy. I have written this testimony to proclaim the good news that Jesus saves!

Here is what her husband has to say in testifying to the faithfulness of God when we answer His call on our lives.

Faithful Is He Who Called Us (Testimony)

As early as I can remember, I was plagued with a poor self-image. Being a perfectionist by nature, I had always put lofty expectations on myself but could never really meet them. The goals I did achieve never quite filled the void. Up until age fourteen, I was driven to get straight A's in school and excel in sports. Still, I was not the person I wanted to be, and with the pressure of being a teenager, I needed something that would work, so I tried alcohol and drugs.

Although people liked me and I had a lot of friends, I didn't like myself. Somehow I was convinced that alcohol and drugs were the answer to my problems. From the start, my drinking and drugging became a daily ritual.

After ninth grade, I had quit sports, lost interest in study, and had a new crowd of friends. Smoking marijuana during the day and drinking at night and heavily on weekends became the order of my life. As I progressed through high school, speed, psychedelic drugs, cocaine, etc., were now in the picture. I was still empty inside but was convinced I would find the answer in the right drug.

I graduated high school by the skin of my teeth, and at age eighteen, I was free to do what I wanted. Alcohol and drugs topped my agenda. By this time, I knew alcohol was not the answer. I'd binge on whisky and vodka and finally ended up with bleeding ulcers. Quaalude and Valium was the next so-called answer to my turmoil. Eating twenty to thirty pills daily, I had turned into a zombie. I was fortunate to be alive after a binge, which included being run over by a pickup truck, almost drowning in a lake, and driving my car off the road.

I was smart enough to know I couldn't continue this way of life, so I started using narcotics instead of alcohol and sedatives. At first, I abused prescription drugs like Percocette and cough syrups obtained by using phony prescriptions, but soon my addiction progressed to Dilaudid and heroin. Once again I thought I had found the answer but was soon under the seemingly unbreakable bondage of shooting dope daily. Trouble came through credit card fraud, armed robberies, and finally getting caught.

I had been arrested a few times for possession, and just days before Christmas of 1983, I was arrested with two others for armed robbery of a convenience store. I remember thinking in the jail cell that night, *How did my life become such a mess?* I was bailed out by my family and entered the first of three rehab programs. I can clearly remember the day when complete hopelessness set in. I thought to myself, *I cannot stop using drugs, and I am going to die if I don't stop.* Because I grew up Catholic, I knew there was a God; and though I did not have a personal relationship with Him, I asked Him to help me. It was at that time that I completely surrendered; thus, it marks the day of my freedom from drugs and alcohol, January 10, 1984.

For the next three years, I would be searching for the truth and the meaning of life through means of the twelve-step programs, A.A. and N.A.

The first few months of sobriety were scary. I thought I could not live without drugs. I kept hearing from the counselors at the treatment center I was in that I wasn't going to make it. This made me determined to make right decisions. I knew going back to using drugs and drinking meant death. After a month of sobriety, I went to a place called Marathon House. This type of program is known as a therapeutic community or concept house. I didn't know what to expect, but was assured I wouldn't go to jail if I stayed in the program. To make a long story short, I was living with a troupe of hard-core addicts trying to reform the old habits and personalities without the power of God. I decided to leave there and take my chances with the courts. I clung to the hope that by making right decisions and seeking God I would make it.

The next two and a half years, I was heavily involved with A.A. and N.A., and the A.A. big book was my Bible. My life seemed to get better, and God spared me from going to jail. I met a woman in the program and got married. We both sought a relationship with God and trusted Him for our lives.

However, God was still abstract. He wasn't personal. I still had a tremendous emptiness in my life. Looking for spiritual answers outside the programs, I focused in on a New Age, Eastern religion-type meditation. I somehow thought I could reach sinless perfection and this would please God and soothe my guilt-ridden conscience. But, although I was now three years clean and sober, the more I fell short of the standards I set for myself, the more frustrated I got.

Around this time, big changes occurred. I had been married for two months when I decided to move from Boston to Providence, Rhode Island, to work for my father. God used this move to take me out of the circle of the A.A. and N.A. meetings and program friends. I started trying out meetings in Providence, and for some reason, it seemed like they were clouded with spiritual darkness. (Also at this time, I wanted to find a church for myself and my family. I didn't want the same old ritualistic, denominational church I grew up in.) I agreed to go to a church a friend of mine had been attending in Framingham, Massachusetts. I heard a great message, met some loving people, and received Jesus Christ as my personal Savior. When I did, a burden was lifted off me. What was "impossible for me was possible with God" (Mark 10:27).

My family and I attended church in Johnston, Rhode Island, the next Sunday, and I heard God speak clearly to my heart: "This is what you've been searching for all your life." It was amazing. All the years I did drugs, all the years I sought God in A.A. and N.A. programs culminated in the fact that finding Christ in the local assembly, having a pastor/teacher, and being part of the body of Christ was the answer. I began to sense an eternal purpose for my life and soon was attending three church services per week, going soul winning, and enrolled in Bible classes. I stopped attending A.A. and N.A. meetings. I did not need them anymore.

Seven months later, in answer to God's call, we moved to Baltimore, Maryland, where I entered Bible college. Again we obeyed God and had learned that "faithful is He that calleth you, who also will do it" (1 Thessalonians 5:24).

Now in 1995, it has been eight great years with the Lord, and I have had the privilege of going on missionary trips to Thailand and Las Vegas and helping with the Grace Overcomers Ministry.

Only Christ Can Truly Satisfy (Testimony)

I was born into an amazing Christian family. My parents loved me unconditionally and sacrificed to give me all that they could. They brought me to church three times a week and sent me to a Christian school. Both of my parents had great personal relationships with Jesus Christ and constantly revealed His life to me at every turn. The truth was, while I was a good kid and never complained or got into any serious trouble, I did not have a personal relationship with the Lord. Outwardly, I probably looked like a great Christian kid.

When I was fourteen years old, my parents made the decision to go on the mission field. Of course they took me along. I was greatly excited to be going to Europe and was taken by the adventure of it all. There was no doubt in my mind that I was born again. However, when temptation reared its ugly head, I became vulnerable. I was vulnerable because I could not see the great life that everyone was talking about. I could not seem to grasp it for myself.

Hanging out, I sought companions of the same mindset, doubters and scoffers. I began drinking and smoking weed. My parents caught me and confronted me. While I expressed sorrow outwardly and swore that I would never drink or use drugs again, inwardly there was no true repentance. Consequently, I continued sneaking around, drinking, and smoking at every opportunity.

Back home, after a year in Europe, I took up with carnal friends, looking for other options than what the church had to offer. We all seemed to have a hunger to know a life other than the one we had.

For the next three years, I continued drinking and drugging at every opportunity. During this period, I began to realize that I was spending all this money and time and I was totally depressed and dissatisfied. I was going nowhere and had no relationship with God. One night, alone in my room, I began to cry out to God, "Lord, get me out of this situation. I want more out of life than this emptiness." I knew this could not be the reason I was living on earth.

Not remembering the prayer the next day, or week for that matter, I continued doing what I was doing and not enjoying it. About two weeks later, while riding in a car with some companions, we got pulled over and busted for possession of drugs. I remember thinking that my life was over. My parents would kill me! In the middle of this thought, God spoke to my heart and said, "This is from me. If you will take it from me, I will put you in a large place. If not, this will be your place in life, and it will only get worse."

As a result of this incident, I was expelled from school in my senior year. I sought out Pastor Dan Lightsey of Grace Overcomers and met with him on a weekly basis. Pastor Dan spoke faith to me and encouraged me in the Lord. I was able to graduate from high school at the end of the year.

Upon graduation, I took a year off and was seeking admission to a college. I even put a deposit down on one I was accepted by. All the while, however, I knew deep down that God was calling me to Maryland Bible College and Seminary. I resisted signing up but found that as I attended, God was doing a great work in my life. He had put my feet in a large place. Every day I am amazed at the life I now have, living for and walking with God.

Since that time, I have graduated, gotten married, and I am studying for my ordination. I have honestly found the reason He has put me on this earth. God is so faithful to answer when we earnestly call out to Him. He has given me a new life, a new name, and His righteousness. In exchange, He has taken my old life, my old identity, and everything related to it.

There is nothing on this earth that can satisfy like Jesus Christ.

CHAPTER 4

A Temporary Dwelling Place

God gives clear definition in His Word using the Israelites and their trials, triumphs, and errors as "examples for our learning" (1 Corinthians 10:1–33). He gave specific instruction on how the wilderness tabernacle, and eventually the temple, should be built of which the Christian is a type (Hebrews 8:5, 9:1–28; 2 Peter 1:13–14). God's grace is extended to all. So even those who are not believers benefit from Christianity. Since "all scripture (though written by men) is given by inspiration of God, and is profitable for doctrine, for reproof, for correction, and instruction in righteous living" we can learn a lesson about the twelve steps from the following biblical scenarios (2 Timothy 3:16).

Though the twelve steps were generalized, having the pure gospel message left out of them, they are still biblical principles. The illustration is regarding the twelve wells of water (Exodus 15:27). Here we have a mixed multitude of people out of the twelve tribes of Israel, believers and non-believers alike, being refreshed at the wells. However, they could not quench their thirst at those wells had Moses, God's man (a type of pastor/teacher), not obeyed God and "cast the tree into the water" at the brook Marah. By Moses' act of obedience, "the waters were made sweet," Continuing, he says (and we paraphrase), "diligently hear the voice of the Lord thy God, give ear unto His commandments, keep all His statutes. And God is speaking through Moses when He says, "I will keep you from disease and heal you" (Exodus 15:25–26).

Since there were so many people, human nature being what it is, some of them no doubt scoffed at Moses. They would have quenched their immediate thirst and then run from the scene of the twelve wells. They would have not continued to drink the water, but instead would have wandered off in the wilderness and died, their thirst never having been thoroughly quenched.

The message was too simple; it was an insult to their intelligence. By this method, they were not in control of their own destiny. To them, the tree, a type of the cross of Jesus Christ, would have been an offence, a stumbling stone to their lifestyle (Romans 9:33; 1 Peter 2:8). The second group would have worshiped the tree, making it their higher power. They would have loved the tree, but they would not have internalized its true message. When it was time to move on, they would not have trusted God for the journey. They also would have "died in the wilderness" (Numbers 14:32).

The third group is in the book of Joshua. The waters of the Jordan River are raging. There is no natural way that the people can cross the river because it is at flood stage. Yet Joshua says to them, "Sanctify yourselves, set yourselves apart, prepare your hearts, confess your sins, tomorrow the Lord will do wonders among you" (Joshua 3:5).

In this instance, God gives specific instructions to Joshua on how the crossing, a supernatural work of God, is to be undertaken. Here there were twelve stones in the midst of the Jordan River, which Joshua commands the priests to take out of the waters of the river, carry over to the lodging place, and leave as a memorial (Joshua 4:7–8). Notice he does not tell them to carry the twelve stones on their journey to the promised land. Can you imagine the weight of the burden?

A lodge refers to a temporary dwelling place, not a permanent home. Yet some people spend their entire lives in twelve-step home groups, religiously working their way up the steps, hoping to have a spiritual awakening. As a result of grace, some do.

CHAPTER 5

Forty Years in the Wilderness (Testimony)

Here is the story of one whom God brought out of just such a wilderness by grace alone.

My addiction began in 1941, with the occasional smoking of my father's cigarettes. Shortly thereafter, at the coaxing of the older boys in the neighborhood on Chicago's northwest side, where I grew up, I began sipping his beer and taking a slug of the whiskey that he kept on the pantry shelf for special occasions.

Along with drinking and smoking, I began stealing money and lying in an attempt to cover the thefts. No one told me to steal the first time or to lie; it seemed to come naturally. Money brought a certain sense of security, recognition, and acceptance among my peers. I felt that as long as I had a glow on and a wad of cash in my pocket, things would be all right. Somehow, though, like a mirage one sees on a hot desert highway, the illusion never materialized.

My father, though honest and hardworking, was an alcoholic. In his frustration with me for being expelled from school and the turn of events in my life, he would verbally abuse and physically assault me in an attempt to knock some sense into my head. Though I know he loved me, he was impatient and inconsistent in his discipline. My mother had died with postnatal complications when I was ten days old. While my stepmother was patient and loving toward me, I was resentful and abusive to her. All in all, my parents were good material providers. My father's life did, however, change dramatically years later when he turned to the Lord.

Enrolled in parochial school at an early age, I was indoctrinated into Catholicism. Religious training, while giving me a Christian foundation for which I am forever thankful, nevertheless caused me to form legalistic concepts of God that did not have a grace premise. Unable to live up to the standard put before me, conflicts arose within my soul. Fueled by an awakening sex drive, those conflicts caused an inner confusion, which seemed to enhance, rather than quell, my rebelliousness. Threats of hell, while striking terror in my heart, had no lasting effect on my behavior.

Sociologists and psychologists sought out by my parents, and appointed by the juvenile court, had a field day recording and analyzing the psychosocial data surrounding the events in my early life. Needless to say, they never arrived at any sound conclusions as to what should be done. Without going into a diatribe of symptomatology and self- analysis, it is sufficient to say that I had a serious problem.

A year spent with my aging aunt in Mississippi, enrolled at St. Aloysius Military Academy in Ohio, and finally a year at Gibault School in Terre Haute, Indiana, all at great expense to my parents, did not change me.

The increasing use of alcohol, amphetamines, and the smoking of marijuana during my early teenage years caused havoc. Brief periods of abstinence were plagued by feelings of rejection compounded by fear, insecurity, and guilt.

At seventeen, I began injecting heroin daily and quickly became addicted, supporting my habit by the stealing and refunding of merchandise at department stores. The geographic cures initiated by my family were of no help. A stint in reform school, county jail sentences, psychiatric hospitalizations, and incarceration in the Oklahoma State Penitentiary at McAlester did nothing to dissuade me from self-destruction. I did not intentionally set out to destroy myself, but a continuing series of wrong choices was taking its toll.

During many incarcerations, I read books on psychology, philosophy, and religion, along with medical and psychiatric case histories, in a quest for life's meaning and to enable me to get one over on the medical profession.

By my mid-20s, I had become a scoffer at the mention of God's name. I was a young man who hated authority. I blamed God for my mother's untimely death and my family's rejection of me. I possessed no work skills, never held a job or paid taxes, and was totally consumed with the obtaining and using of opiate drugs. Whenever arrested, I would feign mental illness, displaying a variety of psychotic symptoms in order to avoid criminal responsibility. Toward the end, I had even convinced myself that I was crazy. Operating outside of societal norms and standards, I did whatever it took to keep myself medicated. My rationale was this: that I did what I did in order to cover my emotional pain.

Saved from a Hollywood Career by a Life of Crime

In 1965, I was sentenced to the federal penitentiary at Leavenworth, Kansas, for fifteen years. I had robbed a Hollywood bank on a whim one day, in an effort to continue feeding the elephantine drug habit that had overtaken me.

At the time, I had aspired to be an actor, associating with the characters on the fringes of the film capitol. Possession of a ready cache of drugs earned me the awe and respect of my cohorts. Some of them were well known jazz musicians and entertainers. As a result of my being able to supply drugs to them, I was readily accepted in their social circles. Seemingly, they held me in high esteem. Now forsaken by them all, I sat in that cold Kansas cell with the fifteen-year sentence the judge had given me hanging over my head.

Looking for answers, I began attending weekly Jewish services in the prison conference room. I was fascinated by the Jewish customs and traditions and greatly admired the Jews' seeming ability to prosper in the face of adversity. For me, a return to Christianity was out of the question. My anger toward my parents and rebellion toward the God of my childhood prevented me from any consideration of the Jesus of my youth. In my warped way of thinking, Christianity seemed corny and contrived. It did not fit my intellectual mold; neither did it mesh with the mentality I had adopted in the haunts of Hollywood, which I frequented. The atmosphere in the coffeehouses of San Francisco's North Beach had not been conducive to my embracing its simple message either.

One night, though, as I lay alone in the darkness of my prison cell, unable to sleep, the Holy Spirit began to speak to my heart. "Your parents were right, the Sisters of Charity and the Holy Cross Brothers were right. You should have listened to them. If you had, you wouldn't be where you are right now." *Was this the Jesus whom I had turned my back on as a little boy, whom I had mocked as a teenager?* The thoughts going through my mind were having an effect. I almost started talking to God that very night. However, the devil countered with old convict line, "You didn't pray on the street; why start now?"

I had mouthed responsive Hebrew prayers in the Jewish services on Saturday afternoons, but I was not yet ready for dialogue with God. A preoccupation with legal motions in the federal district court to vacate my sentence squeezed any immediate consideration of Jesus Christ from my consciousness. I had become a jailhouse lawyer of sorts, and through my effort had miraculously won an early release from prison, another manifestation of grace and mercy extended to me throughout my life.

Though saved from a life of crime, I continued to live in carnality.

Leaving Leavenworth, I returned to the west coast just in time to join the hippies. On my thirty-first birthday, October 7, 1967, I met a pack of ragamuffin evangelists who were part of the Jesus movement. They told me of God's love for me and my need of salvation. At their bidding, I made a sincere profession of faith. In the serene surroundings of San Francisco's Golden Gate Park, I accepted Jesus Christ. At the time, I was homeless. They took me off the streets, allowing me to stay in a mission they maintained in Marin County.

For the next several months, my drug use was reduced to the drinking of table wine, the smoking of pot, and the occasional tripping on LSD. I was able to rationalize these indiscretions with the same fuzzy logic that I had always depended upon in the past.

While those fledging Haight-Ashbury Christians extended an abundance of love and grace to me, there was no sound doctrine taught from the Word of God; nor was there any accountability to a local church.

As a result of my continuing drug use, I wore out my welcome at the mission. Back on the needle, I was again tearing up and down the coastal highway, chasing the ever-elusive dream. Within weeks, I was arrested on a possession charge. Awaiting trial in the Los Angeles County Jail, I read the new testament from cover to cover. Several times over, I read, "God is love" and had a revelation of His unconditional love for me in spite of my drug addiction (1 John 4:8). Hitting the streets again that spring, though, I was beset by my cravings and quickly resumed my old habits. Tiring of jail, I made it to New York's East Village in pursuit of the now legally obtainable drug methadone.

Upon getting saved, I ceased from overt criminal behavior. I was, however, still living in what I now realize was gross carnality.

The next five years were spent on various methadone maintenance programs. No longer able to feel the effect of opiate drugs, I became addicted to alcohol, drinking up to a fifth of whiskey a day. When I couldn't get that, I guzzled cheap wine. Cocaine was becoming readily available, and I developed a voracious appetite for it as well.

Over the years, my body became riddled with needle scars. Had it not been for intermittent jail terms, for various drug charges and hospitalizations, I would have no doubt annihilated myself.

Adept at faking medical symptoms, I was able to keep myself supplied with narcotic prescriptions. But the more drugs that I did, and the more alcohol that I drank, the less I found solace in these substances.

A physician, sympathetic to my cause, had admitted me to the hospital, at my request, in an attempt to decrease the mammoth amounts of the drug Dilaudid that I had been self-administering for so long. It was during that hospitalization that I met Pastor Bob White.

A Renegade Christian

I told Pastor Bob that I was a believer in Jesus Christ but that I was also an addict and would probably never be able to stop using drugs. I called myself a renegade Christian. Although saved, I had lived for fourteen years, taking grace as a license to sin. Having a grasp of situational ethics, I had rationalized over and over again the depth of my rebellion and denied the power of God to deliver.

According to a story I once heard, W.C. Fields, the Hollywood actor, was found reading the Bible one day on a movie set.

A fellow actor asked him, "What is a drunk like you doing reading that?"

"Just looking for a loophole," Mr. Fields was reported to have said.

Addicts always look for the loopholes. One of my favorites was to accuse Christians of being hypocrites. I had formed a distorted concept of Christianity, which conjured up images of people, especially leaders, living in perfection. When they failed to live up to my standard of righteousness, I labeled them phonies. I was the phony! Of course I needed to be loved, but in my fear of rejection, I would erect walls of weirdness, such as shaving my head bald just prior to attending Pastor White's church for the first time. I did this to alienate people so that they could not hurt me, or even worse, uncover my defense mechanisms and thus make me accountable to truth.

Pastor Bob befriended me, not making an issue of my strange behavior or the fact that I was still doing drugs. He never judged me; he only told me of God's love for me and revealed His grace by his own personal testimony, along with an unswerving attitude toward me. He showed me the way through preaching loving messages on the power of the cross and God's promises of deliverance.

Pastor Bob was the Moses who, true to the biblical scenario spoken of earlier, presented the cross to me. The Lord shows Moses the tree (a type of the cross), which, when he had cast it into the waters, the waters were made sweet (Exodus 15:23–25). Through Pastor Bob's ministering to me, I began to have a vision of the bitterness of my life being made sweet. Like the woman Jesus met at the well sin had given me "pleasure for a season" but could not satisfy my deepest desires, one of which was to be set free from addiction (John 4:7–26; Hebrews 11:25).

Shortly thereafter, a couple in the church took me into their home, where I was attempting, with their help, to wean myself from the habit. They and Pastor Bob had invited me to attend a church convention in a neighboring state. Prior to leaving their house, I had taken a leap of faith, flushing hundreds of dollars worth of Dilaudid down the toilet. I struggled through withdrawals up to the last night of the convention, at which time a healing service was held. Touched in the service, I proudly proclaimed on the P.A. system before a crowd of over 2,000 believers, "God has healed me of withdrawal symptoms and a life of addiction."

Upon returning to Vermont, however, I slipped back. In the absence of a living faith, my sobriety was short lived.

One night, several months later while attending an A.A meeting (my father had introduced me to A.A. when I was a teenager), I ran into an old salt named Pastor Bill Hill. Bill had been introduced to me at the church convention I had attended. A retired executive and a regenerated alcoholic, his ministry was to prisoners at the Berkshire County House of correction in Pittsfield, Massachusetts. Coincidently, I had been locked up there on a couple of occasions.

As I sat in that meeting, sweating over a cup of coffee and the effects of 200 milligrams of orally ingested methadone (enough to medicate a team of horses) Pastor Bill's steady gaze penetrated my sin-sick soul. At that moment, deep inner conviction cut me to the quick.

At his invitation, I consented to meet with him the following day for coffee. At that meeting, he exhorted me to "get some guts," and labeled me a "first-class jackass." With deep, piercing eyes, and in brokenness, he told me, "God could use a man like you." He also told me all my friends were waiting for me at the cross.

"Ahhh," he scoffed angrily, dismissing me, "you don't have the character it takes to live sober."

He was right. I had been totally lacking in character throughout my entire life. I left our meeting wounded by his words.

Months later, I was to read Proverbs 27:5–6: "Open rebuke is better than secret love;" and "Faithful are the wounds of a friend."

My addiction was not just to drugs; it was to a lifestyle and all the trappings surrounding it. I had been having this idolatrous love affair with "lady amapola" (Spanish for opium poppy) for many years. She was a predictable and jealous woman who wielded power over me. Like the addiction process Dr. May refers to in his book, she had "nailed my affections and enslaved my desire." *Amapola* had been more than willing to allow me indiscretions with *ethyl* (the chemical name for alcohol), but she could not co-exist with this church crowd.

Essentially, this stronghold of Satan was not to be easily broken. I was like the simpleton in Proverbs 9:13–18 who sleeps with the foolish woman, thus sinking to the depths of depravity and depression. Though the fear of sober living was very real and powerful, the fear of dying a hopeless drug addict was even more frightening. Worse was the fear that I might not be saved from an eternity in hell if I continued in addiction. Since I had read in Galatians 5:2 that "drunkards do not inherit the Kingdom of God," I was not going to take any chances.

The Christian, who is truly saved, may, because of free will, choose to live in addiction or any other overt sin. Sin, in my opinion (based on a multitude of scriptures and the nature and character of God), does not cause one ever to lose his salvation. However, the Christian who continues in sin will be miserable, in line for chastisement, and will ultimately die the sin unto physical death.

In Identification with Jesus Christ

As I sat in my rented room, in an old, Victorian house on Summer Street in Springfield, Vermont, loneliness took its toll. Chain smoking one cigarette after another, searing my lungs along with my sin-sick conscience, I cried out to God with the same pain that the Apostle Paul must have felt in Romans 7:24, when he said "O wretched man that I am who shall deliver me from this body of sin and death."

Pastor Bill's challenge echoed in my ears. Thoughts of all those people from Pastor Bob's church kneeling in prayer at the foot of the cross flooded my heart. In my mind's eye, I could see them waiting patiently, beckoning me to come. It was on that night in early September of 1981 that I came to the end of myself. I was standing on the banks of what was to be my own personal Jordan River experience.

True to the biblical scenario in the Book of Joshua, chapters 3–4, God sent a *Joshua* to me in the form of

Dr. Carl Stevens. He had presided over the convention I had attended earlier that year.

Someone in the church had given me a taped message entitled "Certain Certainties," which Dr. Stevens preached years earlier. It was a moving apologetic, defending the veracity of the Scriptures and substantiating the fulfillment of biblical prophecy. I could no longer deny the truth. Every time I was tempted to call my physician for another prescription to alleviate the pain of withdrawals throughout the long nights, I simply played the tape.

Still it was a perilous crossing, perilous because I had to trust God rather than the idols of destruction that I learned to depend upon in my wilderness wandering, which ironically lasted forty years almost to the day.

Christian writers and friends too numerous to name had been an inspiration to me throughout my life. It was through their love, prayers, and investment that I was able to cross over. "Fellowshipping with His sufferings" at the cross of Calvary, in identification with Jesus Christ, I had finally exercised my free will in a positive manner (Philippians 3:10).

Many times I had attempted to do the right thing, make the right choices, and flee from the bondage of my sin. No matter how hard I tried, or who tried to help me, I would ultimately fall back into the pit of addiction. But this time, as the song says, tarrying at the "Old Rugged Cross," I finally let Him take it all, and I have continued to do so daily ever since. The fears, insecurities, and the cravings of my past are now dead; they are buried in the finished work of my Savior, Jesus Christ. I no longer have to overcome my flesh; it is dead. I can now live in the resurrection power of the risen Christ, who sustains me and upon whom I cast all my cares. By His shed blood and abounding grace, and because I am in Christ and He is in me, He has overcome all that which I could not. That is why I am a Grace Overcomer.

Thank You, Jesus, for Setting Me Free (Testimony)

My aunt told me about Jesus when I was a small boy, and I believed. From that day on, God has sent His servants to influence me to stay on the straight road and not to deviate from it, though for a while, I went astray.

I grew up in a small town in Oklahoma with a population of maybe 300 people. A woman named Gwen took care of me while my parents were at work. She was a Christian, and now has a husband and three daughters. Gwen told me that she had prayed to God that if she was supposed to babysit, He would send her a child who would be in His plan. She pulled into a gas station after saying that prayer, and the attendant asked her if she would be interested in babysitting for a woman who had a son and was moving to her town. I was that child.

I had never heard that story, and I was so blessed to know how God planned to place me with a Christian family, since my parents were not practicing Christians. Gwen and Emily would call my house every Sunday morning to ask my dad if I wanted to go to church, and he would then wake me up. I went to church with them regularly. They raised me up in those vital years with godly principles and convictions that would stay with me for the rest of my life.

In my teen years, I faithfully went to church on my own. My parents thought that I had turned into a fanatic. I wanted so much for them to believe what I believed in and for them to go to church with me.

Many times I felt as though I was on a fence, with my parents' world on one side and my babysitter's on the other. As I look back, I see that when I straddled the fence, I always fell on the worldly side. Double-mindedness caused me to compromise.

In my first year of college, I met a Christian, who became my best friend, and we shared our faith. But in my sophomore year, I met a girl, and I took her out to a club to go dancing. I drank some champagne to loosen me up before I went to meet her, since I was so shy. I compromised, saying to myself that it wasn't a sin to drink but only to get drunk. The date was successful, and I asked her to marry me after two weeks. We were married six months later.

I was twenty-one years old and soon realized that we were not compatible, but a baby was on the way. I was so unhappy. Secret drinking and extra-marital affairs began and went on. My relationship with God had been broken because of sin.

At age twenty-six, I was working in a convenience store during the night shift. I asked the woman I was seeing on the side if she knew about a drug called cocaine. It was supposed to keep you awake. She said her brother could get me some. We snorted it, but I said that I was disappointed because I did not experience the great change I had heard stories about. He told me that if I wanted to feel its full effect, I would have to shoot it up. I was hooked after the first shot. It didn't take long until I had lost everything—all my possessions, my wife, and my two children.

I went to a rehab for thirty-five days. Once I was out, I kept on drinking, which eventually led me back to cocaine. My abuse of the drug went on for four more years. God chastised me over and over, but I just would not give it up. Finally, in September of 1991, after a two-day drug binge, my heart was racing, and I thought death was approaching. I cried out to God and told Him that I wanted to give up the life that I was living and I wanted to get back into the fellowship that I once had with Him.

I had become a slave to my sin, and I wanted to be set free. After coming out of the emergency room that night, I checked myself into a rehab in a small town outside of Baltimore, Maryland. There, during one of my classes, I met a man who gave me his testimony. He was a Christian. I told him that I was a Christian too but had been backslidden for ten years. He told me that he was a pastor. He told me about the church he attended and about a meeting that was held once a week called Grace Overcomers. It was a drug and alcohol recovery program based upon biblical principles.

This was great news for me, and today I thank God for sending this man to encourage me. God also added His personal touch, which I thought was phenomenal. In the course of our conversation, I found out that we were both born in the same town in Oklahoma! I knew that God had arranged this divine meeting, just as He had with my babysitter years earlier.

During the Grace Overcomers meetings, I was taught from the Bible that I was not my sin, that I was a new person in Jesus Christ, that every day was brand new, and that the old me was now dead and buried and could remain that way.

Thank you, Jesus, for setting me free.

CHAPTER 6

Circumcision of the Heart

In recent years, twelve-step groups have been heralded as *the* method of recovery for everything from hardcore heroin addiction to food and multiple relationship addiction. Numerous books have been written on accompanying topics such as co-dependency, dysfunctional family, the child within, and so forth. In most instances, these writings are the products of unregenerate thinkers whose premise, if they have one at all, is vague. Addiction is a three-fold, self-inflicted disease of the body, soul, and spirit. Two of those components are in the spiritual realm, so it only makes sense that we have to begin to find the solution to the problem with a sound theological premise.

From the days of Nimrod and the building of the tower of Babel mankind has invented religious programs to reach or appease God and salve a guilt-ridden conscience (Genesis 11:1–9). Recognizing that there are two different kingdoms: that of "darkness and all of its principalities and powers" and that of "light," opposing forces at work and that "a little leaven leavens the whole lump" we must "arm ourselves with truth" lest we fall into serious error (Ephesians 6:12–6:13; 1 John 1:5; 1 Corinthians 5:6; Galatians 5:9).

In summation, there are four types of people in these biblical scenarios who are typical of people who find themselves in twelve-step groups. There is the one who comes to meetings for a while because of pressure from family or an order from the court; however, he never drinks from the twelve wells, and as a result, never really stops whatever it is he is addicted to.

The second person comes and drinks from the wells, worships the tree, or any number of other gods he is introduced to through the writings of New Age gurus, philosophers, (whose works are circulated on the fringes of the movement) or, through meditation, (getting in touch with one's inner self) seeks to self-improve through introspection. By applying a simplified form of Freudian psychology, he re-tells and relives events in which he either wronged others or was wronged. While these efforts, in some cases, produce abstinence from the drug or behavior of choice, the result is usually the switching from one addiction to another. The person also would be considered a non-believer because he has a form of godliness but has never come to a saving knowledge of Jesus Christ. He is in denial of the truth. He, along with those in the first group, dies in the wilderness.

The third type of person attends meetings, drinks from the wells, and in the course of making "searching and fearless moral inventories," and "while making amends," discovers that he is spiritually bankrupt. Many times this person is drawn to sponsors who are believers, such as the Harold and Lamar types, who eventually lead him to the

Lord. He uses the twelve steps as the stones to cross the Jordan River. He is a believer but would be considered carnal because when Joshua gave the order to move on, he was fearful to leave the lodge. He hung around the memorial grounds, reworking the stones (twelve steps) and "feeding on the ashes of the burnt idols" in one another's past experience (Isaiah 44:20).

This practice reinforces this person in who he is in his "Adamic," or addict nature, and precludes him from finding out who he really is in Jesus Christ, where "old things are passed away" (2 Corinthians 5:17). Confessing we are addicts every time when we open our mouths has a negative connotation (and affect on our lives). The Christian is taught to "put off the old man with his former conversation" (Ephesians 4:22).

The result of any work-orientated program (whether it is in a self-help setting or legalistic church) is spiritual death. "The strength of sin is in the law," so a legalistic message (common in many fundamentalist churches) can never be lived up to; thus it condemns the listener and causes frustration and eventually rebellion (1 Corinthians 15:56). On the other hand, those who do seem to live up to such messages outwardly become judgmental, taking on an attitude of self-righteousness. This causes subtle and not-so-subtle pride to take over and results in arrogance. Those who are weak and continue to fail, live in discouragement because they do not measure up. They become insecure and jealous. This causes backbiting and devouring (Galatians 5:15). The human condition is such that the tendency is to "compare ourselves among ourselves." The Bible cautions against this practice, saying people who do so are not wise (2 Corinthians 10:12).

The devil loves religious works programs because they tend to divide people into cliques. But he hates grace! Grace unites Christians, making them a force to be reckoned with. Many times, the self-help models produce cheap grace that is taken as a license to live in sin (Jude 4). We are exhorted to "stand in true grace" (1 Peter 5:12).

God does not call the addict out of addiction to hang around the lodge but to a life of faith obedience. In the Joshua scenario, those "men of war who obeyed not the voice of the Lord were consumed" (Joshua 5:6). The Bible says, "Where there is no vision, the people perish" (Proverbs 29:18). Since we do not war after the flesh, and the weapons of our warfare are not carnal the struggle to overcome addiction in the energy of the flesh is never successful (2 Corinthians 10:3–4). An attempt to do so results in our being consumed or burned out. Thus, we have the dry-drunk syndrome.

This speaks of depending on one's strengths in the Adamic nature. When we were out on the streets, some of us carried knives and loaded pistols. We were liars, thieves, and forgers; hustlers, cunning and crafty. Our hearts were hardened. We were drunk drivers, wife beaters, and neglecters of our children. By the world's standards, we were hopeless cases. By behaving in a deceitful manner, we found that we could arrange circumstances to defend our right to remain addicted. We had learned our lessons well and were masters of the art of manipulation. A tone of voice, a tear, a tantrum, an arched eyebrow, facial expressions (from a frown to a menacing sneer or a winsome smile), body language and exaggerated hand gestures—these were some of the weapons we used to get what we thought would make us happy. They were the character traits we possessed. We were products of our own fractured personalities. These were the defenses we had depended upon in our wilderness experience. Though we had given up the addictive drugs and some of our behavior patterns, we did not, because of fear, abandon these, our carnal weapons. For us to do so, we would have to change our thinking. The lodge mentality would not be conducive to our doing so. In order to accomplish this change, we would have to have balanced biblical teaching.

The fourth type of person is the one who puts himself under that teaching and goes all the way with God. He is like the Joshua and Caleb types who, though they may still attend twelve-step meetings, are committed Christians.

All the men who entered the land of promise that the Word of God speaks of in the Joshua scenario "had to be circumcised by Joshua" (Joshua 5:2–8). This means our sitting under the teaching of a spirit-filled man of God. Those who are circumcised in their hearts identify with the "death, burial and resurrection of Jesus Christ" "put on the whole armor of God" and go forward (Colossians 2:11–13; Ephesians 6:11).

More recently, some evangelical groups have started programs using the twelve-step format. Corresponding Bible verses to fit the twelve steps are used in an effort to introduce those familiar with these programs to Jesus Christ and the Bible. We applaud these efforts and commend anyone who preaches the gospel. However, we would caution against any tendency there might be to self-improvement without making a clear distinction between the old man and the new creation.

Again, let us emphasize that we are not being critical of any program that presents the gospel of Jesus Christ to the lost; however, sound teaching must always follow.

It is our opinion, based on experience, that God, in his permissive will, allowed the twelve-step program to be written, this in spite of the apostate phrase "god as we understood him." We do not believe, as many do, that it is a God-given program, but that God uses people as salt and light within the confines of the rooms and uses the twelve steps to get people dried out so that He can speak to their hearts.

Since many people we encounter are already involved in self-help programs, and that is their primary source of spiritual input, we often find it hard to get people, because of fear, to make the local church their home. It must always be their own choice to do so. If we are willing and prayerfully seek wisdom God will show us where we are to be (James 1:5).

He did for this man, who is now the pastor of a local church. While working on his master's degree in divinity, he is helping others like himself to be grace overcomers.

CHAPTER 7

From the Gutter to Glory by the Grace of God (Testimony)

My drinking and drugging began in the early 70s and was to have a devastating effect on my life. My early teenage years were taken up with alcoholic drinking, pot smoking, and the use of a variety of psychedelic drugs. Somehow, through it all, I managed to graduate from high school.

Joining the military in early 1975, I hoped to escape my addiction. This, however, was not to be, for my thinking and attitude went into the service with me. As a result, I was discharged a year later for my lackadaisical performance of duty.

Upon returning home, one of my friends told me how Jesus had changed his life. I told him I was happy for him, but I would do it my own way. And do it I did.

Around this time, drugs were flooding my hometown, and I began dealing as a means to supplement my unemployment checks. For the next four years, I continued this lifestyle, obtaining welfare when my unemployment ran out. During this time, I was arrested and often spent time in the county jail. Locally, I had the reputation of being burnt out and beyond help.

Moving to Houston, Texas, I found a job and did well for two weeks. A year, three jobs, and three apartments later, I found myself homeless because of my drug use.

A year and a half was spent on the inner city streets of Houston and, eventually, Miami. I survived by working out of daily labor pools for minimum wage and going to various rescue missions at low points for food and shelter. Life on the street was taken up with drinking cheap wine and smoking pot. It was there that I learned what violence, loneliness, and despair were all about. Along about this time, my heart began to be touched by Christian workers and the donations of food and clothing, which I received as a result of their efforts. Still, in my stubbornness, I thought I could get myself off the streets without the help of Jesus Christ.

At Easter of 1983, while visiting my sister in Fort Lauderdale, we watched the movie *Ben Hur*. At its conclusion, she asked me if I really believed Jesus had died on the cross. I remember saying yes.

Back on the streets of Miami the next day, I was robbed at gunpoint for my last three dollars. The following morning, I decided to hitchhike to the Florida Keys and try my luck on the shrimp boats. The first person I met in Key West was a local pastor who invited me over to his house that evening for a barbecue. There were around thirty Bible school students in attendance, who were down on spring break. They sang songs and shared their faith with the homeless and curious who stopped by.

It was on that night that I realized it was because of my sin that I was where I was. I also understood that Jesus loved me enough to die for me and He was waiting right there to enter my life and help me in my dilemma.

The following day, while walking around looking for work, I asked him to be my Savior. Afterward, I found a job washing dishes at a local restaurant. Soon I began attending Bible studies at the pastor's house.

About a week later, he allowed me to move into an apartment with a few other men who were studying God's Word. The first scripture verse I memorized was, "Therefore if any man be in Christ, he is a new creature: old things are passed away; behold all things are become new" (2 Corinthians 5:17). The pastor told me that in God's sight I was not a bum or an alcoholic but his son, whom he loved unconditionally.

As the weeks passed by, I began to write God's promises concerning my life in Christ on index cards: Galatians 2:20; Romans 8:1–3; 1 Corinthians 1:30–31; Romans 6:6, 11, 13; Colossians 3:1–3; and Ephesians 1:3–14. Attending the pastor's church, I made many new friends and began to learn what it meant to be truly loved.

At times, during the next year and a half, I struggled with my past addiction problems, but each time I failed, by God's grace I confessed my sin and quickly returned to fellowship with his Son.

The turning point in the struggle was when I completely turned my life over to the control and direction of God. Since that day, November 2, 1984, I have been drug and alcohol free.

In September 1985, I entered Bible college, in answer to the call of God on my life. I married in 1988, and my wife and I continue to serve God together. Behind any accomplishments that I have made is my Lord and Savior, Jesus Christ, and his abundant grace, along with my brothers and sisters in Christ who have encouraged me by their kind words and deeds. They never condemned me early on when I stumbled. Today, nothing can separate me, or anyone else who seeks him with an addiction problem, from his love (Romans 8:37–38). His will is for me to love my wife as he loves me so that my family may be centered in His grace. Today we attend a local church where we are taught His Word concerning the great salvation that the Son of God purchased for us with His precious blood (Ephesians 5:25). That teaching truly can transform the soul!

"He raiseth up the poor out of the dust, and lifteth up the beggar from the dunghill, to set them among princes, and to make them inherit the throne of glory" (1 Samuel 2:8). This promise has become true in my life. Jesus Christ "hath raised us up together, and made us sit together in heavenly places in Christ Jesus" for all eternity (Ephesians 2:6). It is a place of honor, dignity, perfect acceptance, and holy love. This becomes true for all who receive the Lord Jesus as Savior. May all who read this learn to rest in what He has done; being overcomers, you can "reign in this life as you receive the abundance of grace and live in the gift of his righteousness" (Romans 5:17). Search out the promises of God in Christ Jesus for they are always yes and amen (2 Corinthians 1:19–20).

CHAPTER 8

Positive Volition and the New Position

What Dr. May says in his book regarding grace, and its being the remedy for overcoming addiction, proves true what has been said thus far. We have found that what the Bible says about sinful behavior, and the application of grace in changing that behavior, is true and has been proven by the evidence of the changed lives written about in these pages. Therefore, we can agree with the Apostle Paul, when he says, "Where sin abounds, grace does much more abound" and John Newton, the drunken slave trader who wrote the song, "Amazing Grace" (Romans 5:20).

But what is grace? According to *Webster's Dictionary*, it is "favor, kindness mercy, forgiveness; divine assistance given man for his regeneration (starting life afresh) or sanctification (setting a person apart unto himself with that person's cooperation or willingness)."

In a world where religious systems promote people based on performance, we are conditioned throughout our lives to that mode of thinking. Therefore it is hard for some of us, considering what we have been programmed to believe, to accept grace or understand it.

We do not pretend to be able to cause one to do so in these few pages, since volumes have been written on the subject.

What we desire to accomplish is to give you, the struggling addict, hope, and also to give ministers of the gospel, who are reading this book, sound grace principles from which to operate as they preach, teach, and thus counsel those with addiction problems. As godly counselors and counselees, which we all are, we must operate from the premise that the Bible is the inerrant Word of God. Although written by men, it was inspired by the Holy Spirit (as briefly stated earlier on in our introductory statement) and is God's revelation of Himself, His attributes, character, and nature to the human race. Furthermore, because our Creator is a "God of love," one of his chief attributes—along with holiness, righteousness and perfect justice—"is love" (1 John 4:8). He has given us the Bible as a manual by which we may live in emotional, physical, and spiritual stability. On this basis, we draw the conclusion that all valid counseling must be biblical in nature. "He sent his word, and healed them, and delivered them from their destructions" (Psalm 107:20). Since God is the Creator of the universe and we are his creatures, created in His image to love, serve, and glorify Him (Genesis 1:1, 1:27; Deuteronomy 6:5 Psalm 72:11 Isaiah 24:15. He has a plan for each of us individually, and that plan is perfect (Ephesians 1:11; Proverbs 20:18). It is a grace plan that must be accepted by faith. As we begin to understand God, we must realize that there is nothing we can do in our fallen Adamic nature, or in the works of our flesh, to carry out His plan (Ephesians 2:8–9).

In order to establish that fact, we must go back to the beginning, so as to consider and take into account the rebellion of Satan the angelic conflict spiritual warfare and the fact that Satan's domain is the world, which "lies in wickedness" and in which he has been allowed by God to set up a kingdom that is a counterfeit of, and diametrically opposed to Himself (Isaiah 14:12; Daniel 7:21; 2 Corinthians 10:4; Revelation12:7; 1 John 5:19). Drug addiction is a result of our being influenced by that kingdom. At this point, we should ask ourselves why a loving God would allow Satan to do such a thing. The answer is because of His infinite love. All of His created beings were given a free will. This includes us, Satan, and all the angels. In simple terms, it serves God's purpose to do so. He will not violate free will. God did not create robots. Being counseled in the new creation is simply exercising positive volition and learning the value of our new position in Christ.

Here is the statement of a man who lives in just such counsel.

I Don't Do that Anymore (Testimony)

When I was sixteen, my dad passed away. Even though he was an alcoholic, he was a very loving and generous man in many ways. He was the man of my heart.

I was raised up in a dysfunctional home because of alcoholism. My brother and I became substance abusers. After the death of my father, my brother became my male image. Ironically, he himself was in need of one to follow, as his abuse led to his tragic death in a motor vehicle accident. My drinking came to an end three years after his death.

Finding it difficult to hold a job because of my drinking, I decided I had enough. I made an appointment to attend an A.A. meeting. A strange thing happened when I was on my way out the door. The Lord spoke to my heart and said I didn't need the meeting, all I needed was Him. I wasn't saved at the time, but I agreed with Him. I prayed and quit drinking. After two months of sobriety, I came to my senses and received Jesus Christ as my personal Savior.

God's great grace and regular church attendance, a study of the Word of God, and Christian fellowship was the key to my deliverance. Today I lead a group of Grace Overcomers. We had twenty-one people attend last Tuesday evening's meeting and are rejoicing in seeing many of them succeed in getting sober God's way.

Proverbs 28:13 states, "He that covereth his sins shall not prosper: but whoso confesseth and forsaketh them shall have mercy." Confession is great, but forsaking the behavior that created my addiction is greater. The key to my sobriety is thinking with the new mind. "As a man thinketh in his heart so is he" (Proverbs 23:7).

Trying to quit produces much frustration and anxiety. I had to come to the realization I had to give up my adherent behavior. That is the greatest advice I can give a recovering addict—a new life in Christ, a new self-image, brand new behavior patterns, and forsaking the old ones.

Tell yourself in the time of temptation, by the grace of God, "I don't do that anymore!"

When someone entices you to indulge, whether by

Satan through projections, a friend, or family member, just say, "I don't do that anymore." Anything short of that is leaving the door open to failure.

I guess that's my testimony: "I don't do that anymore."

☩

What he does is go into the prisons of Connecticut with the same message. That message gave this man, whose story follows, a new lease on life.

A New Self-image, a New Life, and a Brand New Purpose (Testimony)

It was the most horrible event that took place in my life. All I could remember was coming out of a dazed state and waking to find my hands cuffed behind my back. Sitting in a state trooper's police car, I screamed in pain because of a sharp wrenching feeling in my back. I asked the officer, "What happened?"

He leaned over and shouted in my face, "You just killed two people."

That was six years ago. I can't believe it happened. Here I was, a successful college graduate with a prosperous engineering career, on my way to the top, but *crash!* My alcoholism had finally caught up to me. What seemed like just another few cold ones with the boys led to unspeakable anguish and guilt for the taking of two innocent lives on that cool July evening. A head-on collision, that was totally my fault, destroyed two families' lives. How could I live with that? How could I face the manslaughter charges and a possible ten years in prison?

For many months after this event took place, I seriously thought suicide was the only answer. I went to two psychologists over a period of six months. They taught me how to talk about my feelings, how to breathe properly when I got anxiety attacks, and how to accept myself for who I was. I tried a weekend New Age retreat to try to get in touch with the little boy inside me. All this pacified my emotions, but it did nothing for the real pain, guilt, and sadness I felt inside. People would tell me, "I know how you feel." I always smiled, but inside said, "You have no idea what pain I feel." I struggled with not drinking alcohol. I could feel my body craving it, but my pride wouldn't let me do it. I could not trust myself to drink again. This hurt, because I always turned to my beer bottle whenever things got rough, also when things were going good.

It happened on January 20. I was sentenced to two five-year terms to be served consecutively, a total of ten years. Even more difficult than receiving the sentence was looking into the eyes of the father of the girl I killed, the sister of the man, and numerous others who wanted me dead. All I could do was hug my father and say good-bye as they led me away to serve my sentence.

The first days in prison were very difficult. I won't go into details, but I was extremely scared. However, the second week there, I joined the A.A. group and began to learn about recovery from alcoholism. I found it very informative and could identify with what the others were saying.

The next evening, I was invited to a Christian service. I gladly accepted, not even knowing what *Christian* really meant. I knew it had something to do with

God and Jesus, so I figured it would be a safe place to be. Little did I know that it would be the beginning of my new life. The service was in Spanish with English interpretation. I didn't fully understand what was going on, but I just listened. All at once, a sentence that the pastor read grabbed me: "Jesus said, 'Come unto me, all you that labor and are heavy laden, and I will give you rest" (Matthew 11:28). That's all I heard. It flooded my heart, and in an instant, I had peace that I had never before experienced. That day in the state prison, I accepted Jesus Christ as my personal Lord and Savior. I surely didn't understand it, but I knew that God had touched me.

As I look back now, I see the faithfulness of God to ordain my steps. He brought a man of God into my life, who began to teach me the riches of Christ. The pastor taught me from the Bible and said that I was no longer in prison but in Bible school. He showed me God's thoughts about forgiveness, and I knew I was forgiven. Other portions of God's Word said that I was perfect and blameless in His eyes. What Jesus Christ did on the cross truly finished the work of redemption. God washed me, He will never leave me, and I can never leave Him. Knowing this gave me tremendous victory over my guilt, my alcoholism, and my thoughts of suicide. My pastor preached a message in the prison about 2 Corinthians 5:17: "Therefore if any man be in Christ, he is a new creature: old things are passed away; behold all things are become new." I had accepted that for my life, and it caused me to go forward with God.

It is now six years later. I served two and a half years in jail, and I am graduating from Bible college now. My new wife and I have a vision to be missionaries in South America. Not all was a bed of roses after I became a Christian, but I will say, I learned and continue to learn to think with the mind of Christ. He has given me a new self-image, a new life, and a new purpose. As I see it, the key to victory is hearing the Word of God, being taught in a precise manner, and being part of an active church that has God's heartbeat for people.

CHAPTER 9

The Enemy Is Pride

Because of pride, iniquity was found in Satan's heart and he rebelled against a loving God. Satan also took not only himself, but he took a third of the angels in heaven along with him in rebellion against God. Once he did this, he became the epitome of all that is evil. His goal is to take as many human beings to hell with him as he can. Those who are saved, he cannot take. However, he sets out to incapacitate us so that we will not be effective in carrying out God's plan.

Some time after the fall of Satan took place, God created the first human beings, Adam and Eve (Genesis 2:7, 22). Placing them in a perfect environment (again with free will), He only gave them one prohibition: they were not to eat the fruit of the tree of knowledge of good and evil, lest they die spiritually and, eventually, end their lives in physical death and eternal damnation(Genesis 2:16–17; John 3:18).

Being curious and susceptible to Satan's wiles, first Eve, through the lust for knowledge, then Adam, ate of the forbidden fruit, thinking that it would provide something good. As freewill agents, they disobeyed

God, just as we did, as our stories have told, the first time we entered into illicit relations, drank alcohol, or took drugs. We were programmed to the feeling of pleasure that the sinful activity provided and thus opened up to the consequences of that sin. Had we not known what it felt like, we would not have missed it. Adam and Eve were cursed to the very marrow of their bones, where the blood cells are manufactured; and thus, their sinful nature was passed along to their children and eventually to us.

Therefore, sin resides in our innermost being; that is why it is so hard to break sinful habits, opiate addiction probably being the hardest; because it changes the very cell structure of the human body. It is said that certain lifestyles, such as gambling, the lust for money and power, along with sexual sins, are in the blood.

God in his infinite love, foreknowledge, and wisdom slew animals, and thus by the shedding of their blood, the first sacrifice for sin was made. He then covered Adam and Eve with the skins of those animals. Having a guilty conscience, they tried to hide from God by covering themselves with fig leaves which are the world's covering and will always wither away (Genesis 3:10; Psalm 1:3).

This act of love, on the part of God the Father, typified the work of redemption that would be carried out by His Son, Jesus Christ, on the cross (John 19:30). This work was done in behalf of all humanity for all time (John 1:29). This is grace!

In order to get a glimpse of grace, begin to understand it, and put it in its proper perspective, we would again refer to *The Systematic Theology* of Dr. Chafer (pages 118–120) and quote a few excerpts from the doctrine of human depravity.

"Depravity is what God declares that he sees, and precisely what he sees when he looks at fallen man." Dr. Chafer instructs the student to "give unprejudiced and exhaustive consideration to all that is recorded in the Bible on this theme. He goes on to say, "It means that there is nothing in fallen man which God can find pleasure in, or accept." He further states, "The picture looks dark, and would be darker still, were it not for the divinely provided remedy, which announces full and free salvation." Again, this is grace.

Continuing, Dr. Chafer says that "the unregenerate person as seen by himself and those around him appears to be good." Pride tells us that we are. However, human good and self-righteousness produce a stench in God's nostrils, and thus He likens them to "filthy (menstrual) rags" (Isaiah 64:6).

Satan and the angels that followed him "kept not their first estate" (Jude 6). Even though they had knowledge of God, His kingdom, and ways and had been created and taught by him, they did not adhere to his divine edicts. Satan was jealous of God and so sought to supersede his authority. Contrary to what the old hell inspired song says, there should be no "sympathy for the devil," for he is behind all the sin and suffering in the world. All addiction problems start out with believing his lies.

To begin to understand grace, we must accept our total depravity, the fact that we are lost and can do nothing to save ourselves, and that what Jesus Christ accomplished on the cross when he submitted to the

Father and allowed himself to be sacrificed in our behalf, does save us when we believe. But because we were practicing addicts, living outside of God's plan in a body of sin and death we were at enmity with God (Galatians 6:8; Romans 8:7). In our minds, we could and would not face the facts. At the root of our problems were gross inherent character defects (Job 19:28). These brought about wrong thinking, wrong volitional choices, and spiritual death, resulting in guilt (James 1:13–15).

When the case was presented, many of us in the early stages simply did not believe. Our pride got in the way. The ramifications of living in the cycle of sinful (addictive) behavior and guilt had far reaching effects, ranging from neurosis and sometimes even psychosis in the psychological realm. Physiological illness of many and varied kinds also plagued us. Since we were no longer living in denial of the truth, we realized that every one of us needed a daily intake of Bible doctrine and cleansing of our conscience if we were to be of a sound mind (sober) and aware of the wiles of Satan. If we were not vigilant, we would be "devoured" (1 Peter 5:8).

In equipping ourselves to deal with the enemy, not on his terms but on God's, we would again turn to the Scriptures and quote from those and the *Systematic Theology* of Dr. Chafer.

Satan's Limited Authority

1. *His personality*

    According to Dr Chafer: "As is the case with Jesus Christ, our knowledge of Satan depends wholly on what the scriptures declare."

2. *His power*

    a) "as created his might was second only to God's" (Ezekiel 28:11–16).

    b) "After his moral fall," (Job 2:7; Isaiah 12:14–17; Luke 4:6, 22:31; 1 Corinthians 5:5; Hebrews 2:14) "and even after his judgment at the cross" (John 16:11; Colossians 2:15) "he continues to reign as a usurper" (2 Corinthians 4:4). Dr. Chafer further states that we are to "consider all passages throughout Scripture on Satan's temptations and solicitations to evil."

3. *His work*

    a) "Relative to God, his evil works are still permitted."

    b) "Relative to demons, they must do his will."

    c) "Relative to the unsaved, he is in authority over them" (Isaiah 14:17; 2 Corinthians 4:3–4; Ephesians 2:2; Colossians 1:13; 1 John 5:19).

    d) "Relative to the saved, he comes in conflict with them" (Ephesians 6:11–18).

e) "Relative to truth, he is a liar" and the author of the lie (John 8:44).

4. *His career*

   a) Past
   - "Satan experienced a moral fall" (Isaiah 14:12–17; Ezekiel 28:15; 1 Timothy 3:6).
   - "Satan's judgment was predicted in Eden" (Genesis 3:15).
   - "His judgment was accomplished on the cross" (John 12:31–33).

   b) Present
   - "He is reigning as a usurper today" (2 Corinthians 4:4; Ephesians 2:2; Revelation 2:13).
   - "He gains the name accuser of the brethren" for what he is doing now (Revelation 12:10).
   - "He is the father in a spiritual sense to all who accept his philosophy of independence from God" (John 8:44; Ephesians 2:2).

   c) Future
   - "He is to be cast out of heaven" (Revelation 12:7–12; Isaiah 14:12; Luke 10:18).
   - "He is to be confined to the abyss for 1,000 years" (Revelation 20:1–3, 7).

- (3) "When released from the Abyss, he will lead armies against God" (Revelation 20:8–9).
- (4) His final doom is the lake of fire (Revelation 20:10).

CHAPTER 10

Ultimately It Is God Who Changes Behavior

All behavior outside of God's will is the result of wrong thinking, based on information which was taught from childhood by imperfect parents, teachers, peers, a humanistic or religious educational system, the arts, media, literature, and ethnic, socio-economic and philosophical factors. The information that we receive goes into our memory center and affects the thinking process and the formation of character. Defense mechanisms, or lack of them, determine in part what our personality is going to be like. Either we are transparent and Christlike or guarded and suspicious.

Our Adamic personality is that exterior of each one of us that we choose to put on display, having a different mask (or fig leaf) for every mood and situation, but it rarely reveals our true character. Trials reveal our true character.

There are several classic examples that illustrate this principal of truth. The first is found in Ezekiel 8:12, where God inquires of the prophet, "Son of man, hast thou seen what the ancients of the house of Israel do in the dark, every man in the chambers of his imagery?" The second example is found in Matthew 23:27, where Jesus pronounces woe on the Pharisees when he says, "Ye are like unto whited sepulchres, which indeed appear beautiful outwardly, but are within full of dead men's bones, and of all uncleanness." These are examples of what lies in the recesses of unregenerate minds and carnal hearts and, as a result, is what comes out of our mouths when we are either under pressure or think we are out of the earshot of people. In Matthew's gospel, Peter swore the oath, "Though I should die with thee, yet will I not deny thee." But the trial revealed his true character, when under pressure, he began to curse and swear, saying, "I know not the man" thereby denying Christ (Matthew 26:74).

How many times have we said, "Oh, God, please, just get me out of this one; I'll never do it again," only to find that as soon as we are turned out of the jailhouse gate or cash our paycheck, we are in the bar room or off to see the dope man? All of our oaths go out the window for "the spirit is indeed willing, but the flesh is weak" (Matthew 26:41). In God's economy, it is the fruit of the Holy Spirit that counts. Character is not determined by natural will power but is the product of a new nature. Only the formation of Christ in the soul truly strengthens character (Galatians 4:19).

Thinking and its ensuing behavior can be at best moral, or, at the opposite end of the spectrum, degenerate in nature. We cite Ephesians 2:2–3, 12; Philippians 3:18–19; 2 Timothy 4:10; and James 4:1–5 to back up our premise, further citing Isaiah 1:4–6, 64:6; Jeremiah 17:9; Romans 3:10; Psalm 39:5–6, and chapters 1–3 in the book of Romans to demonstrate mankind's condition, at its best and worst state, outside of redemption. Thus, the battle rages in the soul, causing a conflict which needs to be resolved if we are to live in peace with God and ourselves. The Apostle Paul experienced this when he said, "For what I would, that do I not; but what I hate, that I do" (Romans 7:15).

Counselors who use behavior-modification techniques in the secular realm and various modes of the same in so-called Christian counseling do not operate with these truths in mind when they counsel addicts. Counselors, such as court monitors, probation officers, and social workers, use threats of jail, loss of children, and heavy fines to modify addictive behavior. Even some Christian counseling uses threats of chastisement by God, breakup of marriage, and coerced public confession to make their point. In some instances, using obscure scriptures, preachers threaten loss of salvation. Consequently, they never deal with the root of the problem and, indeed, waste time and exhaust the financial and spiritual resources of those they attempt to counsel. We are not saying that addicts who commit crimes should not go to jail. Sometimes God uses jail (as our stories tell) to bring about humility. Efforts to promote freedom from addiction using behavior modification, more often than not, ends in frustration. Our primary goal, when dealing with the unregenerated addict, must always be to lead him to Jesus Christ. He is the one who resolves the conflict.

The Word of God is a two-edged sword that must go to the root of the problem; thus, it brings about a new way of thinking cutting on one edge, healing on the other (Hebrews 4:12; Matthew 3:5–12).

Saul, the self-righteous religious addict, the murderer of Christians, had to be knocked off his horse (Acts 9:4). God had a plan for his life and began to use him shortly thereafter. As Paul, he still had his struggles with sin, as mentioned earlier (Romans 7). But by being taught finished work doctrine in Arabia (by the revelation of Jesus Christ who separated him from his mother's womb and called him by grace), he overcame. It is this revelation of grace and only this revelation that truly transforms the soul and must be the basis for all Christian counseling (Galatians 1:1–24).

Fearful and impetuous Peter, who denied Christ, though he swore he would not, overcame his fears through Jesus Christ's perfect love toward him, as evidenced by the discourse that took place at the Sea of Galilee (1 John 4:18; John 21:1–25). It was Jesus' unconditional love and total forgiveness of Peter that changed his life.

Our goal, when dealing with the unregenerated addict, is to lead him to a saving knowledge of Jesus Christ and thus begin a process of reeducation that brings about changed thinking, which always involves a volitional choice on the part of the individual. Some of the components that are key to this process are prayer, personal investment, sensitivity to the leading of the Holy Spirit, and His fruit displayed in our own lives (Galatians 5:22–25).

Finally, as mentioned above, a desire and willingness to have God work in one's life is paramount. We cite Isaiah 1:18–20, 55:1; Ezekiel 36:25; and 2 Corinthians 8:1–5 for scriptural consideration. Hence "Christ formed in us" is the only realistic goal (Galatians 4:19). Ultimately, it is only the work of God that changes one's behavior.

CHAPTER 11

The Role of the Local Church in Recovery from Addiction

According to Dr. Chafer's *Systematic Theology* (volume 7, page 127), "the Pauline doctrine of the true and spiritual church is second only in importance to the doctrine of salvation by grace." Watchman Nee, in his book *The Glorious Church,* says, "The work of the church is simply to maintain the Lord's victory." We also refer the reader to booklets, *The Church that Conquers* and *Choosing a Local Assembly,* by Dr. Carl H. Stevens Jr. that cover this subject.

Historically, the church has been responsible for the founding of universities, hospitals, and charitable organizations throughout the world, either directly or indirectly. However, in recent years, the erosion of scriptural values has taken place, and many of those institutions have been taken over by secular humanists. Their intent has been to throw out the God of the Bible, and because of disunity among Christians, they have gone far in doing so.

The approach to the addiction problem has been subject to that same erosion. As a consequence, so called self-help programs have sprung up everywhere. The pastors of local churches have dealt with the addiction problem by reading a few books on the subject, perhaps taking a course in counseling, and/or opening up the church basement to a twelve-step group. If the pastor has convictions, he will speak on the evils of addiction. Rarely will he have first-hand knowledge of the problem. Since addicts come from all walks of life, it would be safe to say that many sit in the pew of the church while they secretly continue the use of their drug or addictive behavior of choice. Whether or not they are saved is a question that only God can answer.

What we have found to be most effective in the gaining and maintaining of sobriety is for one to have a personal relationship with Jesus Christ and to be an active, committed member of the local church. Our stories bear this out. Once we trusted God, came out of the *wilderness* of addiction, and crossed the *Jordan River*, we entered *the land of promise*. This is a type of the local church. In a very practical way, God has provided a refuge for us here. God gives specific instruction through his word on how one is to live and walk with Him and His people on the road to Jericho, where the walls—defense mechanisms that we have erected through the years—are supernaturally destroyed (Joshua 6:5). He further maps out our journey to the eternal city of Zion (Hebrews 12:22–24). It is in the local church where we are united under the authority of an anointed pastor/teacher. Then, God "commands us to be blessed" and the yoke of our bondage is broken (Psalm 133:1–3; Isaiah 10:27).

Taking none of the spoils of our addicted lifestyle, we cast away companions and telephone numbers.

Indeed, everything that connects us to it in any way is "utterly destroyed" (Joshua 6:2). Because we could not in our natural strength "rule our own spirit," we were like a city that is "broken down and without walls" (Proverbs 25:28).

At this point in our lives, we should have a broken heart and contrite spirit (Psalm 34:18). Either we have just come out of the captivity of Babylon, which is like unto a penitentiary that we were hauled off to as a result of our addiction, with our lives in a heap of rubbish, or we are victors of the battle of Jericho (Nehemiah 4:2). In the Babylonian scenario, because we would not put down the idols of our addiction voluntarily, God arranged circumstances to destroy them. This could be the loss of job or driver's license, a jail sentence, broken marriage, homelessness, or hospitalization. In any case, we were candidates for grace. It was in this place that we made godly friends and began to rebuild our lives (Nehemiah 4:1). The local church was where we began to experience the "the fullness of Him" (Ephesians 1:23). By sitting at the feet of the pastor/teacher (a minimum of three times a week) and hearing the Word of God, our faith was strengthened (Romans 10:17).

Since a walk with God is always one of faith and of love, Jesus Christ's love toward us and ours toward others, we receive his grace, which is freely given, and extend that same grace to those we come in contact with (2 Corinthians 5:7; Ephesians 5:2; Matthew 10:8; Romans 8:32; 1 Corinthians 2:12; John 1:16). As we make ourselves available to God and begin to "grow in His grace and knowledge" we learn what it is to have godly friendships that are born in and out of adversity

(Proverbs 17:17; 2 Peter 3:18). Since substance abusers commonly switch their addiction from drugs to sexual promiscuity, we learn how to relate to the opposite sex in purity.

As we begin to have an eternal vision instilled in us and take on the mind of Christ going about the work of God all hell usually breaks loose. It begins with the foxes, those thoughts that invade our minds (Philippians 2:5; Nehemiah 4:6). Negative thoughts can break down the fortress of defense that is being built in our hearts against the onslaught of the enemy (Nehemiah 4:2–3).

There were two central characters in the book of Nehemiah who conspired against the work of God and sought to hinder its progress (Nehemiah 4:8). The first one was Sanballat. In the ancient Hebrew language, this name means *strength* or *stronghold*. This refers to a place in our head that we had given over to Satan when we were practicing our sin of choice. Sanballat represents the chief product of our old sin nature, that stamp of Satan that was put on our innermost desires. It said, "This is mine!" By setting a prayer watch on our hearts, day and night and by casting down imaginations that flood our minds the standard of the Word of God is lifted up (Isaiah 59:19; Nehemiah 4:9; 2 Corinthians 10:4–5). Just as Jesus answered Satan's temptation with, "It is written" we can do the same (Matthew 4:4–11).

The second character was Tobiah. While Sanballat represents the enemy within, Tobiah represents one from without. He usually shows up after we've had an unusually hard day at a new job. He's the old drinking buddy who says, "I just wanted to buy you a drink," or a dope-shooting partner who knocks on our back door with a free shot of heroin. He is a foe that takes on many forms and is backed up by a confederate host of demons, here called Arabians, Ammonites, and Ashdodites (Nehemiah 4:7). They are out to get us to forsake our call and incapacitate us as Christians.

Sometimes they appear in the lyrics of rock music. Though we no longer listen to it or dance to its tunes (if we do, we are foolish), the words were, nevertheless, planted in our heads in time past. The line from an old rock tune told us we were just a brick in the wall. The connotation was that we were just a nonentity that would never amount to anything. While at that point in our lives this was how we felt, we are now "lively stones in a new spiritual house" (1 Peter 2:5). In God's economy, we are VIPs with a purpose. Critics may accuse us of being religious fanatics.

Some of the other common Tobiahs who are used in getting one to discontinue the work on the wall (off the wall remarks) come from the media in the form of everything from subtle attacks on Christianity to false accusations against local churches and fruitful, godly ministries. A number of soul-winning churches making inroads into the devil's territory have been labeled cults in recent years. It is sad to say, some of these evil reports come from so-called watchdog groups who profess to be Christians. Through character assassination, the enemies of the work on the wall "come in the midst of them and slay them in an attempt to cause the work that is being done in our lives to cease" (Nehemiah 4:11).

Certainly, there are cults and false prophets, "wolves in sheep's clothing" and the new Christian should be aware of them (Matthew 7:15). How does one determine if a church is a cult? There are two ways. Number one: A church should publish a doctrinal summary, and if it professes to believe in and adheres to the cardinal doctrines of Christianity, it is not a cult. We test the spirit not by our feelings, or by what people tell us, but by the Word of God (1 John 4:1). Number two: "By their fruits you shall know them" (Matthew 7:15–20). The church should be evangelical (soul-winning). As a result of outreach to all segments of society, its membership should consist of people from all walks of life whose lives have been changed for the better, and as a result, are going about God's business. The church that has a missions program that goes into its Jerusalem, Judea, Samaria, and the uttermost parts of the World will break down racial and ethnic barriers (Acts 1:8).

The praying "Nehemiah-type pastor" will, through the foolishness of preaching speak the truth in love and, by declaring the full counsel of God cause the work on the wall to continue bringing the ungodly counsel of the enemy to naught (1 Corinthians 1:21; Ephesians 4:15; Acts 20:27; Nehemiah 4:15).

A congregation that puts on the "whole armor of God will withstand the wiles of the devil" (Ephesians 6:10–18) and be brought to a full understanding of Ephesians 4. The only times those working on the wall stopped was to take off their clothes for washing which speaks to us of coming daily to God and daily confessing our sin (Nehemiah 4:23; 1 John 1:9). The work on the wall of salvation is appointed by God and takes place within our hearts (Isaiah 26:1). It is the free volitional choice that we make to work out our own salvation with fear and trembling (Philippians 2:12). This does not mean that we are insecure, but that we have a healthy reverence for God.

CHAPTER 12

Though she struggled for ten years, the lady whose story follows continued to come to just such a church. Every time she failed, she washed her dirty clothes and got back up on the wall. She wondered at times if God would ever change her life or take away her pain. One Sunday morning, she found out.

What God Can Do with Damaged Goods (Testimony)

I never had a chance to be a child. We were poor and there were fourteen of us in the family. Although my father made a lot of mistakes, I have yet to see a human being work harder to provide for a family. His job as a butcher in a supermarket was forty miles from where we lived. When the car did not run, which was often, he would hitch rides to and from work. The times he didn't get a ride home, he would walk for miles with two bags of groceries for us. More than once we waited until two o'clock in the morning to eat.

Many winters there would be no heat because we ran out of wood, nor was there proper clothing for school.

My parents were abused as children and brought that abuse into their marriage. Mom and Dad did a lot of fighting. Discipline in our home was harsh and would occur as a reaction to their out-of-control emotions. Sometimes my father would sit alone late at night, and I could see terrible pain in his face. Though he never cried, my mom cried often. Between the two choices, I learned not to cry. My father never drank nor smoked, but my mother had a problem with pills and alcohol. While not a severe problem, it had an adverse effect.

There was incest in my family, and my first sexual experience was at age six and continued against my will until I was about thirteen. I knew that what was happening to me was wrong, but out of fear, I never told anyone. I thought it was just another part of life.

My parents believed in God, and despite all the pain and trouble, they loved us and showed that love in many ways. It went beyond their mistakes. To this day, I know it was their belief in God, which they passed on to us, that weathered the storm.

At fourteen, I ran away from home, as many of my brothers and sisters had done before me. For a while, I moved in with my aunt and got a job near her home. However, my stay with her was short lived, as she had emotional problems as my mother did. Returning home, I continued to work and save money until I was able to purchase my own car and rent an apartment.

Things were going pretty well, when on the way to work, I was attacked, beaten, and raped at gunpoint. Unlike the way some women say you are supposed to feel, I seemed to be unaffected, grateful that I had escaped with my life. Later on, though, I was to realize that pain builds up inside and at some point must be dealt with.

During the next couple of years, I held a full-time job and maintained an apartment of my own. During this period, I began smoking pot and dropping LSD. Timothy Leary preached consciousness through psychedelic drugs. Comedians made records that promoted pot and appeared on TV programs incorporating its use into their routines. While drugs were illegal, law officers turned the other way and winked. Drug use was equated with love and wisdom, and I was looking for both. The impression was that all the enlightened ones were doing it.

Pregnant at seventeen, I found out that the father of my child was a heroin addict and extremely abusive. He said he wanted to do the right thing, swore off heroin, and promised to be good to me, so I married him. After my baby was born, I began to use heroin and cocaine right along with him. Back then we did it just on weekends, managing to work and maintain some semblance of normalcy.

Somehow, miraculously, I was able to keep from becoming addicted through my next two pregnancies. My husband also curtailed his drug use to the point that he was able to finish his studies and get a job as an engineer. Around that time, someone at work introduced my husband to Jesus Christ. He, in turn, led me to the Lord, and we began attending church. The drugs and abuse stopped during this period. However, one day he came home and announced that he had been offered a better job in another city and we were moving away.

We had been attending a Bible-believing church, and I had been encouraged with what God was doing in our lives. When we moved, though, my husband got involved with some people at work and their partying lifestyle. I went right along with him. However, the seed of the Word of God had been planted in me; and though I sold the truth for cocaine, which became our drug of choice, many times over the next ten years, God was faithful to finish what He had started in me.

In some twisted way, I felt if I ran to the pain, I wouldn't hurt as bad as when I ran away from it. In the end, God taught me not to run away from it; with Him I could face it. Although I had been born into a bad life, I realized that my decisions were my own. I could not blame my husband or anyone else for the state I was in, only myself.

The turning point came when I heard a sermon on what God could do with damaged goods. The message didn't take root right away. The gist of it was that I was to sit still and let God love me. We had returned to church, and I would go along well for several months but would ultimately go out and binge on crack cocaine, sinking lower and lower into the pit of depression each time I did so. At four one morning, while sitting on a stoop in the inner city, where drive-by shootings were not uncommon, God met me. Though I had made my bed in hell, He was there, and I knew He loved me.

Prior to this experience, I had an intellectual understanding of God and had been striving to live up to what I thought was an unattainable standard: sobriety on God's terms. And so, I had given up, and consigned myself to a life of drug addiction.

For all those years, I had held onto the pain and anger that I felt. In frustration, I rebelled. Now that I knew that God loved me, I could give it all to Him and begin to love myself. It was at that point that things turned around for me. It was as if angels filled the earth. I had unspeakable joy in my heart, and sitting on those steps, I just let God love me. Shortly thereafter, He gave me these words.

"My Prize"

'Tis you, my love, that gave me birth

Upon this sad, weary, and yet wonderful earth,

Though I have never seen, nor touched you.

Yet I have, for you filled my soul

When I was at my lowest.

My pockets were empty, my integrity waned, and upon me

People looked with disdain.

Yet You lifted me up, and in your name,

Upon a pedestal you put me.

And now your love keeps my heart alive,

Causing me to rise above the sin;

By your grace and mercy, the final prize I'll win.

'Tis you, my love. You are my prize.

Today, my husband and I are serving God with a glad heart. Our marriage, which was tattered and torn, has been mended. God is healing the pain that was caused by my failings and those who were the closest to me.

Isn't it amazing what God can do with damaged goods?

CHAPTER 13

How God, with Our Cooperation, Works

Throughout the pages of the Bible, a loving God in a seven fold divine and progressive revelation reveals his plan to the fallen addict through the death of His Son, Jesus Christ, on the cross (Psalm 19:1; Romans 2:15, 15:4; Exodus 24:12; John 1:14; Hebrews 8:10; 2 Corinthians 3:2–3).

The shedding of his precious blood, in the unlimited atonement makes it possible for us to come to him by faith and receive his free gift of eternal salvation thereby being bought back from the slave market of addiction (John 1:29; Ephesians 1:7, 2:8–9; Exodus 13:14; Romans 8:23; Colossians 1:14; Hebrews 9:12).

At this point, the Holy Spirit fills, seals and takes up residence within us and thus convicts, leads and teaches us to live a transformed life (John 14:26, 16:13; Acts 10:44, Galatians 4:6; Romans 12:2; 1 Corinthians 2:13, 6:19; 1 John 2:27; 2 Timothy 1:14; Ephesians 1:13). Being God Almighty the Creator and Sustainer of the universe, He empowers us to do so (Genesis 17:1, 35:11; Exodus 6:3; Revelation 4:8; Isaiah 40:26–28; Ephesians 3:9; 2 Timothy 1:7; Hebrews 1:3).

Upon hearing this news, some of us are delivered from our old habits instantly, with never any serious desire for them again. For others, it is an ongoing struggle to experience the victory that was won at Calvary's cross, and the addict nature wars for dominion within the soul (James 4:1; 1 Peter 2:11).

We must not be discouraged if we fail in our attempts to live clean. He forgives us when we confess our sin to Him based on His divine justice having been satisfied (1 John 1:9, 2:2). If we submit our will to His and resist temptation we are grace overcomers, because "greater is he that is in us than he that is in the world" (James 4:7; 1 John 4:4). The key to freedom is an attitude of humility; for he resists the proud, but gives greater grace to the humble who live in a "spirit of meekness" (James 4:6; 1 Corinthians 4:21; Ephesians 4:2; Colossians 3:12).

If you want to be set free say, *"Amen!"* Take a step of faith, open the door to your heart and begin with the ABCs (2 Corinthians 5:7; Revelation 3:20). These are seven basic revelatory principals that separate the (spiritual) wise men from the (carnal) fools (Proverbs 9:1–18). Meditate on them! Hide them in your heart! If you do, you will find that you are a pillar in the house of God (Revelation 3:12).

Seven principles or pillars of wisdom

When one thinks of a pillar as part of a building, what comes to mind is marble, a beautiful rock that is formed in the earth from limestone. It is made from the dead fossils of millions of prehistoric sea animals. Marble is, simply put, limestone that has been changed by being subjected to heat, pressure, and pure spring water. Marble's color ranges from alabaster to onyx. It has always been a favorite of sculptors and architects because it is soft enough to work with, yet it is so strong it resists fire.

God calls men and women out of the sea of humanity and the darkness of the earth from every race and ethnic group (1 Peter 2:9; Proverbs 8:4). By our being subjected to heat, pressure, and washing by the pure water of his word, he shapes and forms us. So out of the death of our old Adamic life comes beauty.

Proverbs 9:1 says, "Wisdom hath builded her house, she hath hewn out her seven pillars." We are called of God from the four corners of the world. That call is the result of the Trinitarian counsel that took place before the foundation of the world (Ephesians 1:4). Four and three equals seven. According to *Wilson's Dictionary of Bible Types,* the number seven "is used to represent God's complete provision both in Christ and in His dealings with men. It indicates that character of God, His perfect integrity, equity, and justice."

A pillar is beautiful to look at but has no real purpose when it stands alone. When it is joined with other pillars, it becomes a solid support, an integral part of any structure. Therefore, each of the following seven pillars or principles requires cooperation, a joint effort on the part of ourselves, God, and other believers. The pillars are "the sincere milk, the first principles of the oracles of God" not an end in themselves, but the basis for a new beginning. "Him that overcomes, will I make a pillar in the temple of my God, and he shall go no more out" (Hebrews 5:12; Revelation 3:12). These are the words of Jesus Christ to the addict. The greatest thing that God the Father ever did was to send His Son, Jesus, to die for our sins. The cross is the crux and the central focal point of the universe, the epitome of all wisdom.

1. *Acceptance*

Acceptance is the primary principle. It is our acknowledgement that we are fallen creatures rebellious children, sinful people, that we are "laden with iniquity," sick of head, and faint in heart, and that we need to be healed (Genesis 3:6; Isaiah 1:2–6). In this state, our hearts are deceitful and desperately wicked (Jeremiah 17:9). We were liars to ourselves and those closest to us. When confronted, regarding our addictive behavior, we deny what is obvious to all but ourselves. Acceptance is coming to grips with the root cause of all addiction problems, sin, and the fact that we can do nothing in our natural strength to overcome its bonds (Romans 7:14–24). While self-help programs admit to powerlessness over the substance or the behavior, they do not acknowledge the root cause, which is the fallen condition; nor do they give the remedy for overcoming that condition. They do not tell one what Jesus Christ has done about it.

This brings us to the second phase, acceptance of the free gift of salvation (Ephesians 2:8–9). The minute we accept the gift, we are accepted by God and his people (Ephesians 1:6). A gift must always be accepted.

The third, and last, phase of acceptance has to do with the acceptance of other people—seeing them as God does, without being self-righteous and judgmental. The practice of this principle must be ongoing if we are to understand ourselves, God, and those around us. Titus "accepted the exhortation" of Paul and went to the people of Macedonia (2 Corinthians 8:17). He was sent to the church at Corinth in a time of trouble to restore order. He was used mightily by God throughout his life. Paul presented the Lord's gift of salvation to Titus. He received it and accepted the exhortation to go. Along with Peter and Paul, Titus was one of the first *go* men. Acceptance made him a grace overcomer. We must accept the fact that our addiction is the product of wrong decisions and a fallen human condition (Genesis 3:6; Jeremiah 17:5; Romans 3:10, 23).

2. Belief

Jesus Christ exercised faith when, in His humanity, He went all the way to the cross. When we, by faith, follow Him to that place of death to the self-life, we are victorious. Living by faith is believing in a God we cannot see and trusting that which He says in His Word is true.

As substance abusers, we live in our emotions. Often we say we do not feel as though God is with us. Faith is like electricity; we cannot see it running through the wire, but when we turn on the switch, the light goes on. Our car's engine turns over and starts on the coldest mornings when we insert the key and turn the ignition on. By faith, we believe that the car will start, and most of the time it does. If the car is not properly maintained, though, it will not start, nor will it move. Just as the manufacturer of an automobile provides a manual for the maintenance of a car, God, our

Creator, gives us the Bible. It is his instruction book to us on practical living. If we do not read or hear it and practice it, we will not go forward. We must mix faith with it (Hebrews 4:2).

Living by faith is being persuaded that nothing can separate us from the love of God (Romans 8:35-39). It is believing God in the details of our lives. Having an eternal perspective means we buy the truth and sell it not (Proverbs 23:23). Faith pleases God. If we are to prosper, we must believe that He rewards us when we diligently seek him (Hebrews 11:6). The heroes of the faith were not different than us. They were weak and frail—Noah got drunk, Abraham lied, Moses was a murderer, and David was an adulterer and a murderer. Rahab was a harlot, but by faith she received the spies (Hebrews 11:31). On and on it goes.

When we live in co-crucifixion with him and "by faith of the Son of God who loves us and gave himself for us" our addiction becomes a dead issue (Galatians 2:20). Our belief is in Jesus Christ, who "by grace through faith" provides us with the free gift of salvation, which is the remedy for our condition and is that which causes us to grow (Ephesians 2:8-9; Romans 5-6).

3. Commitment

Jesus Christ was committed to the will of the Father in all he said and did (John 6:38). As a result of his keeping that commitment, "we are not lost, but have everlasting life and shall be raised up at the last day" (John 6:39-40). To many of us, commitment is a scary word. Throughout our lives, we have failed in our commitments to our parents, wives, husbands, brothers, sisters, employers, and best friends. People have failed in their commitments to us, but Jesus never fails, no matter what we do. "He will never leave us, nor forsake us" (Hebrews 13:5).

When we were practicing our addiction, we had given ourselves over to it completely. *Webster's Dictionary* says the word *commitment* means to "entrust or consign for preservation." Jesus said, "He that loves his life shall lose it and he that hates his life in this world shall keep (or preserve) it" (John 12:25). When we turn our lives over to Jesus Christ, he keeps us from addictive substances. The problem we all have with making a commitment is that we try and keep it in the energy of the flesh. This can never be done.

The word *commit* means to entrust with confidence our old life, which has been relegated to the grave. Colossians 3:3 says, "For ye are dead, and your life is hid with Christ in God." Yet we dig up our old life because we do not trust Him in a time of crisis.

Because people have made a commitment to God to pray and visit hospitals and jails and to befriend us, our addictive behavior patterns have been broken. Will we now make that same commitment?

We were committed to the devil's program, and he destroyed our lives. Now we are to "set our affections on things above, not on things on the earth" (Colossians 3:2). We are instructed to "mortify (or put to death) our deeds" (Romans 8:13; Colossians 3:5). Addictive substances and behavior are no longer for us. If we think that they are, we will fail. However, if we seek God and get His mind on the subject, we will no longer have a problem. Our commitment to the plan of God is five fold and consists of daily prayer, meditation on His word, church attendance, Bible study, and Christian service (soul-winning) for which we are rewarded.

4. Dependence

As practicing addicts, we are dependent on our drug of choice. We had become so acclimated to its effect upon us that we had to have it. The fallen human condition is such that deep within us is an inherent fear of death and deep-rooted insecurity. In order to compensate for the way we feel, we tend to set and achieve goals for ourselves so that we may gain the recognition and praise of our parents, teachers, and peers.

As children, we are dependent on our parents to take care of us. As we grow up, we are introduced to our drug of choice and, after a period of time, become addicted. We seek to fill the void within us. In our pursuit of security and significance, we identify with our peers, adopting the mode of thinking, dress, and mannerisms of those in our particular group. Our speech is seasoned with the slang of the group. In an attempt to be independent of our parents, we become rigid in our nonconformity. In the process, we are conformists to the code.

As we approach puberty (this is the time that most of us start experimenting with drugs and have our first sexual experience), we seek to identify with those of our own age group. Many times we enter into worship of those slightly older than ourselves who seem to be successful at whatever they do. We become dependent on their approval of us. In order to gain that approval, we allow ourselves to be subjected to all kinds of rites of passage, among them, sexual exploitation and drug use. If our appearance is such that we are not physically attractive, we do whatever we have to do to gain the favor of those who are in leadership positions.

By the time we come to the end of the road and seek God, we have been through years of prostituting ourselves, lying, cheating, and stealing to maintain. We come to God and his people with tarnished self-images plagued by sin and guilt. It is at this juncture, in our process of Christian growth, that we are vulnerable. If we have been opiate addicts, depending on how far we went, we have usually exhausted all our capital in the form of friends and family. If our wives or husbands haven't left us by this point, they are ready to do so. Once one is addicted to heroin, it take years before the habit is broken; sometimes the addiction is never broken. Our stories have borne out this truth. Cocaine addiction is bad if not worse. When suddenly our drug of choice is no longer available to us, we become very insecure. It is here that we must learn to trust God and His Word.

The danger is that we will switch our dependency from drugs or alcohol to people. Since our emotional growth has been stifled for years, we must be careful not to form ungodly attachments. At this point, some of us rush into marriages that are not in the will of God. What is in order is learning to function in the local church. We must switch our dependency from chemicals and sinful behavior to God.

Often, we think that because we are in the church, among Christians, people are perfect. This is certainly not the case, because the church is full of sinners. In line with the parable of the "wheat and the tares" some people may not even be saved. We are never to presume that anyone who professes Christ is not saved; however, this could be the case. Only God knows who is and who is not His. So we are instructed in God's Word to "know no man after the flesh" nor to trust in the arm of the flesh (2 Corinthians 5:16; Jeremiah 17:5). Many times, because of our insecurity, we tend to seek those who are like ourselves and have similar weaknesses. We should make friends with those who are spiritual and never expect too much from anyone, lest we get wounded and use that as an excuse to relapse. We must learn to "stand in grace" and depend not on people, nor the substance of addiction, but on the "promises of God which in Him are yea and amen" (Romans 5:2; 2 Corinthians 1:18–24).

5. Examination

To examine is to search out a matter by using a standard. In our natural state and when things are going well (or so we think) we do not seek God. Only when the trial comes do we turn to Him. When we are addicts, He (because people are praying for us) arranges circumstances so that we will call on Him and thus be saved. "God knows the secrets of the heart" (Psalm 44:21).

Further on, in the same portion of scripture, the Israelites are crying out to God in their affliction saying their souls are bowed down to the dust and their bellies cleave to the earth (Psalm 44:24–25). Their plea is that he will redeem them "for mercies sake" (Psalm 44:26).

Once we are saved, God the Holy Spirit searches us out so that He may continue to accomplish the work in us that has been started. The method is undertaken by Him in a quiet manner; and, in order for Him to carry it out, we must be still. This work is done in the deepest recesses of our soul. The Prophet Elijah did not hear God in the "wind, the earthquake, nor the fire, but in the still small voice" (1 Kings 19:11–13). Each day we must come before the Lord early. It is there in our moment of quiet contemplation that He will reveal Himself to us (Psalm 63:1).

Examination is carried out in our thought life, not subjective need or "inordinate affections" (Colossians 3:5). The grid under which we operate is "the peace of God, which passeth all understanding, shall keep your hearts and minds through Christ Jesus" (Philippians 4:7). Is what we think based on "truth, honesty, justice, purity, love, good report and virtue" (Philippians 4:8)? These seven pillars are seven checkpoints. Paul said the Philippians were to do that which they had learned, received, heard, and seen in him. First, we are followers of Christ and those men and women God puts in our lives. Those who challenge us to grow in the Lord are our models. The test is always: Is that which we are hearing really His voice? Or are we allowing our emotions, our wants and desires in the flesh, or our bellies to hear for us. If we are transparent before God, He will teach us in His ways. Like the marble of which the pillar is made, we will be easily worked.

When one thinks of examination, usually it is associated with the act of confession. The danger is that we will become introspective and, in the process, our conscience, which is a fallen part of the soul, will condemn us (1 John 3:20). The standard for examination must always be the Word of God. Otherwise, Satan will have a field day, accusing us from morning until night, and thereby making us miserable. We must always "stand in grace" on the fact that "there is now no condemnation to them that are in Christ Jesus" (Romans 5:2, 8:1). Our look inward must always be based on who God is (the almighty one), what He has done for us (died for our sins), and who He has made us to be (His children). Examination of our progress is undertaken by allowing "the word of Christ to dwell in our hearts richly, thereby testing our thoughts and motives" (2 Corinthians 13:5; Colossians 3:16; Hebrews 4:12).

6. Forgiveness

Many of us come to the proposition of recovery overloaded with burdens. What people have done to us and how we have disappointed others often causes emotional pain. Jesus said, "Come unto me, all you that labor and are heavy laden, and I will give you rest" (Matthew 11:28).

When we take on our new identity and begin to think with the mind of Christ we are called to take on His heart of forgiveness, which is that of the Father (Philippians 2:5). When Jesus was on the cross, in spite of his having been scourged, mocked, spit upon, crowned with thorns, and crucified, his words were, "Father forgive them for they don't know what they do" (Luke 23:34). It is not natural for us to forgive others, yet we are required to do so. But pride gets in the way. Our prayers' answers are conditioned on our forgiveness of others. Just as our being forgiven is also based on that same forgiveness (Mark 11:25–26).

One of the grace overcomers, who writes his testimony in this book shortly after he had been saved, was kidnapped by several men from a motorcycle gang. While they held him hostage, he was severely beaten with the butt of a pistol. When they found out they had taken the wrong person, he was released. However, at the end of the beating, when the final blow had been struck, he says that he looked into the eyes of his attackers and in his heart forgave them. He could not do so without the mind of Christ.

Richard Wurmbrand, the Romanian pastor who wrote the book *Tortured for Christ*, was falsely accused and imprisoned for fourteen years. In one of his lectures, he stated that he had been haunted, for a time after his release, by bitterness. Eventually, he was able to forgive his captors.

God forgives us seventy times seven (Matthew 18:21). Knowing that God has paid the penalty for our sins—past, present, and future—and written His laws on our hearts and minds, we know that we should not sin. But if we do sin, the Father forgives us when we confess to Him and, in application of the precious blood of His Son, He purges us from guilt and its effects on our conscience. He remembers no more. In humility, we are required to accept His forgiveness, forgive others, and forget the negativity of the past, living in the fruits of (repentance) a changed mind (Psalm 51; Lamentations 3:23; Hebrews 8:10–12, 9:14, 10:22; 1 John 1:7–9).

7. *Gratitude*

Simply put, gratitude is having a heart attitude of thanksgiving for what God is doing in our lives. It is the principle of faith rest in the finished work of Jesus Christ. No treatment on the subject of gratitude, the root of which can be traced to grace, would be complete without considering Genesis 2:2–3, with the emphasis on verse 3, which says, "And God blessed the seventh day and sanctified it because, that in it, He had rested from all His work which He created and made."

The following excerpts from Dr. Chafer's *Grace the Glorious Theme* illustrate this line of thinking. He says, "the Sabbath under the law was a day; the Sabbath under grace is a life." He continues, "the law even of the Sabbath, was but a shadow of good things to come but Christ is now the substance." He goes on to say that Hebrews 4:1–16 is the full revelation concerning the Sabbath under grace.

The whole message of how God works is summed up in Hebrews 4:9–10, where it says, "There remaineth therefore a rest to the people of God. For he that is entered into his rest, he also hath ceased from his own works, as God did from his." There is no reference in these Scriptures to the rest the Christian enters into at death. It is rather for we who believe enter into rest. Dr. Chafer goes on to say, "It is the rest of him that works not, but believes on him that justifies the ungodly" (Romans 4:5) and the rest of one who, walking in the spirit, discovers that he no longer fulfills (gets true satisfaction from living in the addictive behavior patterns) the lust of the flesh but enters into the realization of the provision through the indwelling Spirit that the whole will of God is to be fulfilled in us, not by us." This takes it totally out of the realm of works. God then, through the indwelling Holy Spirit, (with our cooperation) begins and completes His work in us (Philippians 1:1–6, 2:13; Ephesians 2:10). The result is always a changed heart, which is followed by good works.

For this we are grateful.

For a drug addict or an alcoholic, Sunday (the Sabbath) is the most miserable day of the week. For those of us who were dependent on pharmaceutical drugs, it is a day when doctor's offices are closed and drug stores are either closed early or are not open. We drove hundreds of miles seeking sympathetic emergency room physicians to prescribe for us. Alcoholics wake up on Sunday morning with the shakes and need a drink, and liquor stores, due to blue laws, open late, or in some locales, are closed altogether. The cocaine addict has squandered Friday's paycheck by Sunday and spends the day guilt-ridden and beset by his or her cravings for more of the drug. Heroin addiction presents another dilemma in that most people are home with their families, so those addicts who depend on burglary for their fix money are thwarted. How many of us have sung "Gloomy Sunday" to ourselves as we wallowed in self-pity, dope sick and despondent?

Now that it is over, there is a reason to rejoice! We are about our Father's business! Going to church, paying our vow to stay sober before the congregation, giving our tithes and offerings to the Lord, spending time with our new found family, grateful that we, who were once hell bound, are now heaven-sent as His ambassadors. We keep our eyes on eternity seeking to do His will (Proverbs 13:17; Matthew 6:33; 2 Corinthians 5:20; Philippians 3:14)

Now that you have read these principles, stand in them on the following doctrines. They will take you far as you begin your new life with God in control.

SEVEN REVELATORY PRINCIPLES

Set on Fifteen Foundational Bedrocks of Jesus Christ

GRACE OVERCOMERS

1. Acceptance of the condition:

    Creation revealed His:

G*lory*

   And we agreed that we had fallen short of it. Though we may have abstained from addictive substances and behaviors for a season, the struggle to maintain self-control left us empty. At odds with our Creator and fellows, we sought Jesus Christ for…

Reconciliation

   (Genesis 3:6; Psalm19:1; Luke 1:71; Romans 3:23, 5:6–11, 7:19; 2 Corinthians 5:18–19; James 4:4).

2. Belief in the provision

> Our conscience bearing witness to the truth, we acted on the...

***A**uthority*

> Of the Scriptures, the power vested in Jesus Christ to provide the free gift of salvation to all who come to Him by faith. And in response to His...

***C**alling*

> On our lives, we believed, making His...

***E**lection*

> Of us sure.
>
> (Genesis 22:8; John 5:27; Acts 16:31; Romans 2:15; 8:30; Ephesians 2:8–9; 2 Peter 1:10).

3. Commitment to the plan.

> Jesus said, "If you love me, keep my commandments." He calls us to love, serve, and glorify Him, and with our...

***O**bedience*

> We experience the...

***V**ictory*

> That He won for us; and He graciously conforms us to His image. Our commitment consists of the following:
>
> a) Daily prayer in partnership with Him

b) Meditation on His Word to change our thought life

c) Bible study for our learning

d) Church attendance for our edification and instruction in ...

*E*cclesiology *(Corporate Body Truth)*

And ...

e) Christian service (Soul winning) for which we get temporal benefits and eternal ...

*R*ewards

As an incentive to do His will.

(Deuteronomy 6:5; Psalm 4:4, 5:3, 72:11; Proverbs 16:3, 20; Isaiah 24:15; John 14:15, 15:10; Acts 7:38, 19:32, 41; Romans 16:26; 1 Corinthians 15:57; Galatians 3:23–25, 4:9; Ephesians 1:11; 2 Timothy 2:15, 3:16; Hebrews 10:25; 1 John 5:4; Revelation 2:10).

4. Dependence on the promises:

All of the Scriptures are for our learning, and therein are contained more than 7,000 promises, which through patience and comfort give us hope. Central to them all is the one Jesus Christ kept when He went to the ...

Cross

Which doctrine, when applied to our lives, delivers us from addiction on a daily basis. Therefore, we no longer indulge in addictive behavior or substances but rely on Him. He further promises to...

Ordain

Circumstances so that His life and resurrection power may be made manifest in us, causing us to carry out His will, which brings us fullness of joy and peace of mind (Psalm 37:23, 119:133, Proverbs 16:9; Jeremiah 10:23; Matthew 16:24; Luke 14:26; John 15:11, 16; Romans 4:21, 8:28–39, 15:4; 2 Corinthians 1:20; Galatians 2:20; Philippians 3:10; Hebrews 6:12, 11:33, 12:2; 2 Peter 1:4).

5. Examination of the progress:

We examine ourselves daily in the light of who Christ is, the fullness of Grace and Truth, and what He has done for us. By His...

Mercy

He saved us.

He has made us to be His children. And using His life as our example, we ask ourselves, are we willingly allowing His government to abide in our hearts through love? Are we becoming more like Him (Psalm 139:23; Lamentations 3:40; John 1:14; Romans 5:5; 2 Corinthians 13:5; 1 Peter 2:21)?

6. Forgiveness for the failure:

   Because He has paid the penalty for our sins, past, present, and future, and has written His laws on our hearts and minds, we know that we should not sin. But if we do sin, the Father forgives us when we confess to Him, and in application of the precious blood of His son, He purges us from guilt. We then, in humility, are required to accept His forgiveness, forgive others, and forget the negativity of our past, living in the fruits of (repentance), and a changed mind (Psalm 51; Lamentations 3:23; Hebrews 8:10–12, 9:14, 10:22; Philippians 3:14; 1 John 1:7–9).

7. Gratitude for the result:

   Grateful that we, who were hell bound, are now heaven sent as His ambassadors, we keep our eyes on…

*E**ternity*

   And as He produces His…

*R**ighteousness*

   In us, we rejoice in our permanent and progressive…

*S**anctification*

   Revealing His glory.

   (Leviticus 21:8; John 17:12; Romans 8:4, 2; 1 Corinthians 3:2–3, 5:20; Ephesians 5:26; Philippians 3:12–15; Hebrews 10:10–14, 13:1–15).

APPENDIX

Seven Precepts

We are a loving, outstretched hand of the universal body of Christ to those struggling with addiction throughout the world (Psalm 98:1; 1 Corinthians 12:12). With a hearing ear and a heart of wisdom and understanding through intercessory prayer and by speaking the truth in an encouraging voice of exhortation, we have become the teachable, released from the throes of addiction (Isaiah 59:1; 1 Kings 3:12; 1 Timothy 2:1, 6:2). Here are seven precepts by which we allow God to govern us as His trusted servants.

1. *Unity of purpose*
    - For the sake of unity and continuity of purpose, which is to win the lost and introduce them to the local church, where they will be equipped to live in the truth of Satan's defeat, Grace Overcomers shall come under the authority of Jesus Christ, as He lovingly reveals Himself in the Scriptures.

- So as not to be distracted from what God has called us to do we avoid disputes over sectarian differences, we are not a debating forum. However, we are willing to quietly discuss our positions on secondary doctrines of the faith after the meeting (Psalm 133; Matthew 28:18–20; Mark 1:22, 11:28–29, 27; Ephesians 4:1–32; Philippians 2:14; 1 Peter 3:15).

2. *Fellowship in the light*

    - We do not preclude ourselves from fellowship with any Bible-believing group or individuals; nor do we judge them based on written and spoken reports, or sight evaluations. Our fellowship is around the broken body of Jesus Christ and is based on love, fruit, and common agreement on the cardinal doctrines of Christianity (Psalm 50:4–6, 119:63; Matthew 7:1–5, 15–20; Acts 2:42, 14:1–4; Romans 2:16, 14:13, 16:17–18; 1 Corinthians 1:9, 10:20–21, 13:1–13; 2 Corinthians 5:7, 6:14–17; Galatians 6:1–10; Ephesians 5:1–21; Philippians 2:14, 3:12–20; James 4:11–12; 2 Peter 3:16; 1 John 1:7–9; 2 John 6–11; 3 John 1–11).

3. *Autonomy with accountability*

    - Each Grace Overcomers' group shall be self-governed. Whenever possible, we seek affiliation with like-minded local churches and ministries. In such cases, we submit to the authority of the table of organization set up by the overseeing pastor of that assembly. If there is not a like-minded church in the area, and a sober person has a burden for the struggling addict, he may, by permission of Grace Overcomers, set up a group. In such cases he will be held accountable to the tenets of Titus 1:5–9.

4. *Headship by delegation*

- Each Grace Overcomers' meeting shall be presided over by an elder of the church, or his delegate, and that person shall meet the requirements of that office as set forth in the Scriptures (1 Timothy 3:1–13).

- Women delegated to do so may set up meetings to address issues particular to women, in accordance with the Word of God (Titus 2:3–5; 2 John 1).

5. *Stewardship of finances and the oracles of the faith*

- A secretary/treasurer for each group shall be appointed and records kept of all administrative and financial transactions. These books will be open to the membership, and a monthly verbal account given after the meetings.

- A free-will offering will be taken at the end of each meeting to provide for the operating expenses of the group, such as literature, refreshments, etc.

- Tokens of growth, such as miniature crosses and crowns, may be provided (as expenses permit) as milestones on the road to recovery. These typify rewards that the believer receives at the judgment seat of Christ (Romans 14:10; 2 Corinthians 5:10).

- Since we strive to speak the things that become sound doctrine at the meetings, realize that a little leaven can blow things out of proportion and that a false balance is an abomination; therefore, all literature and tapes sold at meetings shall meet the approval of Grace Overcomers, Inc. This is done as a covering for the new Christian (1 Corinthians 5:6; Galatians 5:9; Proverbs 11:1, 20:2–3; Titus 2:1).

6. *Members in particular*

    - All who seek freedom from the bondage of addiction through biblical truth may be members. All that is required is that one show up at a meeting and be willing to listen with an open mind. Those family members and friends affected by the addictive behavior of their loved ones, and all in the local church, are members in particular (John 8:31–36; Proverbs 12:15; Romans 12:5; 1 Corinthians 6:15, 12:12; Ephesians 4:25, 5:30).

7. *Confidentiality as a covering*

    - The individual member's right to privacy shall be respected. Their names and what they say at meetings regarding the nature of their problems shall not be repeated. This includes verbal and written prayer requests.

- As believer priests, we all have the right to stand or fall before God without being judged (Psalm 32:1–2, 85:2; Romans 4:7; 1 Peter 2:1–25).

Our invitation to those who have read this book is to receive Jesus Christ in your heart. If you have not already done so, say this prayer:

Addict's Prayer

Dear Heavenly Father, I agree with what you say in your word regarding my condition and now accept what your Son, Jesus Christ, did for me on the cross. Save my soul and empower me to live in these principles, free from the bondage of addiction. Amen.

If you have done so, great! Get a Bible and start reading daily in the Gospel of John and the book of Romans. Find a local church, and you will begin to grow. You are like us, a grace overcomer!

If after reading this material your heart has been touched and you would like to start a Grace Overcomers' meeting in your area, you may do so by obtaining written permission from: danlightsey@graceovercomers.org.

Visit our Web site at:
www.graceovercomers.org

BIBLIOGRAPHY

Addiction and Grace. May, Gerald G., M.D. Harper and Row Publishers, 1985.

Alcoholics Anonymous Comes of Age. Alcoholics Anonymous Publishing, 1957.

Choosing a Local Assembly. Stevens, Pastor Carl H. Jr. Grace Publications, 1984.

Grace the Glorious Theme. Chafer, Dr. Lewis Sperry. Zondervan Publishing House, 1922.

Systematic Theology Volume 7. Chafer, Dr. Lewis Sperry. Dallas Seminary Press/Zondervan, 1948.

The Church that Conquers. Stevens, Pastor Carl H. Jr. Grace Publications

The Glorious Church. Nee, Watchman. The Gospel Book Room. *Vine's Expository Dictionary of New Testament Words.* Macdonald Publishing Co.

Wilson's Dictionary of Bible Types. Wilson, Walter Lewis. Wm. B. Erdman Publishing Co., 1957